|The Seven Churches

Tom Stolz

www.bluedoorgeneration.com

|The Seven Churches

Generation Publishing, Portage, Michigan 49024

www.bluedoorgeneration.com
tomstolz.podbean.com

Cover Photo: Charlotte Tancin (1913 Postcard Freeland, PA)
Edited By: Samantha Stolz

ISBN-13: 978-0692341872 (Generation Publishing)
ISBN-10: 0692341870

Samantha, you are my best friend, confidant, hero, and wife. Thank you for always being there. This message has cost you much. I pray it also blesses you, as you have blessed me by carrying it with me and sometimes for me. I love you.

Table of Contents

Chapter 1 – Introduction

One of the most troubling observations I have witnessed in our hour of history is this: I don't know many church leaders that do not agree that we are in the end times, however, I can find few that are teaching what the response of the Church should be in the years leading up to the return of Jesus! This is disturbing, because Jesus' return is REALLY important to Jesus!

The Bible is actually weighted in information about the last 7 years of human history leading up to the return of Jesus. Hundreds of chapters are in the Bible describing what to look for (watch), what and how to pray for people, families, churches, cities, and nations (Pray), and how to get you, your family, and your city ready (Be Ready). Every time Jesus spoke of His return, He warned His disciples to do these three things: watch, pray, and be ready. Jesus' return is not a passive event for anyone, but Jesus wants His Church ready. To not be ready is to suffer much loss. Jesus said He is coming like a thief! Thieves steal. You suffer loss when the thief comes secretly. Jesus said "be ready...I am intentionally coming like a thief"

Matthew 24:42-51 "So you, too, must keep watch! For you don't know what day your Lord is coming. 43 Understand this: If a homeowner knew exactly when a burglar was coming, he would keep watch and not permit his house to be broken into. 44 You also must be ready all the time, for the Son of Man will come when least expected. 45 "A faithful, sensible servant is one to whom the master can give the responsibility of managing his other household servants and feeding them. 46 If the master returns and finds that the servant has done a good job, there will be a reward. 47 I tell you the truth, the master will put that servant in charge of all he owns. 48 But what if the servant is evil and thinks, 'My master won't be back for a while,' 49 and he begins beating the other servants, partying, and getting drunk? 50 The master will return unannounced and unexpected, 51 and he will cut the servant to pieces and assign him a place with the hypocrites. In that place there will be weeping and gnashing of teeth.

Maybe you think "I am ready, Tom." Great! I actually doubt this is true (not to be mean, I don't consider myself ready yet, either), but let's imagine you are ready. According to the Bible, you have an obligation as one saved by Jesus to be talking to others to get THEM ready. "Ready" doesn't mean ready to be a "strong Christian," or die, or get raptured, or some vague notion of "hanging in there," but rather ready to endure the specific events of the end times in victory! How can you teach these if you don't study them?

Did you know the Book of Revelation is describing the most victorious time the Bride will ever see on earth prior to the return of Jesus?! If the Church really believed this, and really believed we were living in the last days, it is all we would talk about. Do you hear the crickets chirping?....chirp...

The truth is, we have lost this reality that Paul and his friends lived in. It was already starting to slip away when Paul wrote to the church at Thessalonica, which was why, once again, Paul was writing to remind them:

1 Thessalonians 5:1-11 Now concerning how and when all this will happen, dear brothers and sisters, we don't really need to write you. 2 For you know quite well that the day of the Lord's return will come unexpectedly, like a thief in the night. 3 When people are saying,

"Everything is peaceful and secure," then disaster will fall on them as suddenly as a pregnant woman's labor pains begin. And there will be no escape. 4 But you aren't in the dark about these things, dear brothers and sisters, and you won't be surprised when the day of the Lord comes like a thief. 5 For you are all children of the light and of the day; we don't belong to darkness and night. 6 So be on your guard, not asleep like the others. Stay alert and be clearheaded. 7 Night is the time when people sleep and drinkers get drunk. 8 But let us who live in the light be clearheaded, protected by the armor of faith and love, and wearing as our helmet the confidence of our salvation. 9 For God chose to save us through our Lord Jesus Christ, not to pour out His anger on us. 10 Christ died for us so that, whether we are dead or alive when He returns, we can live with Him forever. 11 So encourage each other and build each other up, just as you are already doing.

The truth is, understanding Revelation gives vision to put on restraint, like an Olympian training for victory, to get ready. If you have no vision, you cast off restraint. This is what Proverbs says:

Proverbs 29:18 Where there is no revelation, the people cast off restraint; But happy is he who keeps the law.

Now think about this proverb for a minute: Jesus didn't accidentally pick the wording of this verse, and Jesus didn't accidentally name the Book of Revelation the "Revelation of Jesus Christ." This is a direct admonition to know Revelation so that you will be restrained (focused) and joyful in the time of Revelation unfolding. But you don't have to go all the way back to Proverbs to see this. Revelation says it, too!

Revelation 1:3-4 Blessed is he who reads and those who hear the words of this prophecy, and keep those things which are written in it; for the time is near. 4 John, to the seven churches which are in Asia: Grace to you and peace from Him who is and who was and who is to come, and from the seven Spirits who are before His throne,

So John delivers a message from Jesus to the "seven churches." The Book of Revelation is about the time of the end…The seven churches are the end time church. This is what Daniel was told about much of the same information John was given. The Book of Daniel is the Old Testament Revelation of the end time:

Daniel 12:4 "But you, Daniel, shut up the words, and seal the book until the time of the end; many shall run to and fro, and knowledge shall increase."

OK, any 40-year-old to 70-year-old like me and my parents knows that WE are the generations that have seen the knowledge explosion of the internet in our lifetime. My kids don't know this…the internet has always been around for them. My grandparents don't know it, they have never logged on. We are the ones that Daniel was talking about. It is no coincidence that the 70 years olds were just being born as Israel was re-established as a nation for the first time in 1,800 years. That was a nuclear explosion of prophetic fulfillment. The whole nation that was founded on Jesus was supposed to respond in fasting and praying. But, we went in the total opposite direction, choosing materialism and the accomplishments of men instead. That has left us in an unfortunate position. We started thinking Church is about OUR satisfaction with Jesus, rather than about Jesus' satisfaction with us! We must repent, turn off the tube, and get about our Father's business. The "thief" we love is at the door:

Revelation 3:19-21 As many as I love, I rebuke and chasten. Therefore be zealous and repent. 20 Behold, I stand at the door and knock. If anyone hears My voice and opens the door, I will come in to him and dine with him, and he with Me. 21 To him who overcomes I will grant to sit with Me on My throne, as I also overcame and sat down with My Father on His throne.

It is our responsibility to know and connect with this stuff. We are living in the hour all of creation has longed to see. We are the Church of this hour, and friends, we are mostly in La La Land about what is transpiring all around us. This is a life or death thing. For real. It is time to wake up. Now. While there is still time. I believe there is very little time left to get ready. It is time for a cram session, because, by the signs in the earth, the final exam is not just already on the calendar, it is this afternoon and we are still out to lunch with our friends.

Since I have started teaching Revelation, I have found that you get more revelation AS you teach Revelation. Everyone should teach it. You don't need a microphone or church building to teach Revelation, you've got Facebook, your family, family gatherings, lunch with friends...you get the point. Jesus, the greatest preacher of the gospel ever, mostly taught his 11 best friends and one shady character who was stealing the money. God strategically picked those 12 because He knew who they knew. Read and teach Revelation to those around you.

The truth of the hour we live in is that the TRUE great ones that are emerging don't care at all if they are famous, they are actually most satisfied in making Jesus the reward for what they do. The old paradigm of people "making a name" for themselves is quickly going out the door. We all hate the fake self-centered "ministers," and as trouble increases, they will either repent or be shut out. For real. We all might as well start agreeing with that reality right now. A pure and spotless Bride is all that will stand, which means the great ones will be the HUMBLE ones. Your seminary degree won't matter, or your law degree...the ones who will lead the Bride to victory will admit that in the family that will live for trillions of years, we are all just infants. Unless you become like a child, and listen to those who are childlike in their humility, and their main and plain understanding of the Bible, you aren't making it through the next 7 years...period:

Mark 9:35-37 And He sat down, called the twelve, and said to them, "If anyone desires to be first, he shall be last of all and servant of all." 36 Then He took a little child and set him in the midst of them. And when He had taken him in His arms, He said to them, 37 "Whoever receives one of these little children in My name receives Me; and whoever receives Me, receives not Me but Him who sent Me."

Matthew 18:3-5 and said, "Assuredly, I say to you, unless you are converted and become as little children, you will by no means enter the kingdom of heaven. 4 Therefore whoever humbles himself as this little child is the greatest in the kingdom of heaven. 5 Whoever receives one little child like this in My name receives Me.

Right now, many "theologians" have so complicated the simple Word of God, they literally cannot see the forest through the trees. God's Word is given to all men...not just the few that went to seminary or are friends with those the crowd thinks are powerful. Being powerful is of no value in God's kingdom...being submitted to Jesus and the sometimes strange way He does stuff...that is the highest value.   Being taught by men is not nearly as valuable as being taught by the Spirit of the Word. At home, in your pjs, drinking coffee, anyone can be a true MDiv in God's kingdom, it just takes desire:

John 6:45 It is written in the prophets, 'AND THEY SHALL ALL BE TAUGHT BY GOD.' Therefore everyone who has heard and learned from the Father comes to Me.

Luke 10:21-24 In that hour Jesus rejoiced in the Spirit and said, "I thank You, Father, Lord of heaven and earth, that You have hidden these things from the wise and prudent and revealed them to babes. Even so, Father, for so it seemed good in Your sight. 22 All things have been delivered to Me by My Father, and no one knows who the Son is except the Father, and who the Father is except the Son, and the one to whom the Son wills to reveal Him." 23 Then He turned to His disciples and said privately, "Blessed are the eyes which see the things you see; 24 for I tell you that many prophets and kings have desired to see what you see, and have not seen it, and to hear what you hear, and have not heard it."

If those guys were blessed at the beginning of the coming of Jesus, how much more blessed are we to see the fullness of the times, and all the promised signs that come with it.

The promised blessing in Revelation 1:3 to "read," which means to read the prophecy to anyone willing to listen to you, and to "keep" which means to make choices to agree with what you understand the main and plain text to command, is what releases great understanding. Great understanding then brings you into great joy as everyone else is confused. Joy is what God wants us to walk in, no matter what is happening around us. God wants us to be LIKE Him. He is truth and joy. If you understand the truth of what is happening, you will have great joy. Pretending the truth isn't true actually steals your joy, and confusion takes its place.

Revelation is the most positive book in the Bible. The only trouble is, it is also the most negative book in the Bible. It is both. Some teach only the negative stuff, and this leaves the hearer and the teacher growing in the false impression the only solution is for Jesus to remove everyone that loves Him or can hunker down long enough, wipe out the rest, and start over. Nope. Wrong answer. Confusion will be the fruit of that teaching.

Some teach only the positive stuff. This leaves the hearer and the teacher growing in the false impression that things will just get better and better until we make it so nice here Jesus just can't resist us…errggg….Nope…Wrong again. Confusion will be the fruit of that teaching, too.

The TRUTH is the NARROW ROAD. Revelation describes the maturing of righteousness (wheat) and evil (tares). This is super simple. Jesus has never changed His story. Why do so many teachers change His story?!

Jesus told this parable so everyone would understand:

Matthew 13:24-30 Another parable He put forth to them, saying: "The kingdom of heaven is like a man who sowed good seed in his field; 25 but while men slept, his enemy came and sowed tares among the wheat and went his way. 26 But when the grain had sprouted and produced a crop, then the tares also appeared. 27 So the servants of the owner came and said to him, 'Sir, did you not sow good seed in your field? How then does it have tares?' 28 He said to them, 'An enemy has done this.' The servants said to him, 'Do you want us then to go and gather them up?' 29 But he said, 'No, lest while you gather up the tares you also uproot the wheat with them. 30 Let both grow together until the harvest, and at the time of harvest I will say to the reapers, "First gather together the tares and bind them in bundles to burn them, but gather the wheat into my barn." '

Then, Jesus explained the parable to eliminate ANY confusion:

Matthew 13:36-43 Then Jesus sent the multitude away and went into the house. And His disciples came to Him, saying, "Explain to us the parable of the tares of the field." 37 He answered and said to them: "He who sows the good seed is the Son of Man. 38 The field is the world, the good seeds are the sons of the kingdom, but the tares are the sons of the wicked one. 39 The enemy who sowed them is the devil, the harvest is the end of the age, and the reapers are the angels. 40 Therefore as the tares are gathered and burned in the fire, so it will be at the end of this age. 41 The Son of Man will send out His angels, and they will gather out of His kingdom all things that offend, and those who practice lawlessness, 42 and will cast them into the furnace of fire. There will be wailing and gnashing of teeth. 43 Then the righteous will shine forth as the sun in the kingdom of their Father. He who has ears to hear, let him hear!

The wheat and tares are both maturing at the same time. Can't you see this all around you? Isn't this just simply plain? Sin isn't getting better -- murder, theft, sorcery, sexual crimes, human trafficking, war, greed, hunger, homelessness, joblessness, riots -- I don't know about you, but it looks to me like the tares are getting taller. But, SO is the wheat! Night and day prayer is blossoming globally. Unity is being released in profound and miraculous ways. The Body of Jesus is taking baby steps out of the church buildings and trying to reconnect with people. Facebook and the internet are teeming with truth about Jesus, and pictures of half naked women and men, wheat and tares. The weeds grow without any help, but we have to cultivate the desired crop. This is intentionally simple, friends. God wants us to understand and respond.

So, if the maturing of the wheat and tares plain to see, we have to say "Ok Jesus, what else, specifically, did you mention in this parable?" There are three important observations to make:

First, the crop planted by Jesus, the Son of Man, in the gospels, and watered with that first rain in Acts 2, should be maturing. We should see the same crop, later in the season.

So, the question should not be "what did the latest teacher say God wants?" It should be "What did those 120 seeds planted in the upper room experience?"

Persecution? Check; Signs and wonders? Check; Thousands saved at a time? Check; Praying night and day in one accord for power to come so they could go out and do the stuff by first abiding (John 15) in Jesus? Check! We should be maturing in their experience, not changing the game plan to be world domination by infiltration of the seven spheres of culture. This is simple. Acts 5 decribes the best moment in the early united Church . We should be maturing in all these realities:

Acts 5:12-17 And through the hands of the apostles many signs and wonders were done among the people. And they were all with one accord in Solomon's Porch. 13 Yet none of the rest dared join them, but the people esteemed them highly. 14 And believers were increasingly added to the Lord, multitudes of both men and women, 15 so that they brought the sick out into the streets and laid them on beds and couches, that at least the shadow of Peter passing by might fall on some of them. 16 Also a multitude gathered from the surrounding cities to Jerusalem, bringing sick people and those who were tormented by unclean spirits, and they were all healed. 17 Then the high priest rose up, and all those who were with him (which is the sect of the Sadducees), and they were filled with indignation,

Second, satan planted tares in the field. There is bad stuff in the harvest field, right next to the wheat. There is false teaching in the Church. Pretending this isn't true, isn't helpful. Once you start to see them, you cannot miss them. They are super easy to spot, and they are in many places. This is what you look for: bad fruit. They teach stuff that sounds really spiritual and powerful, but they live self centered lives, a lot of the time their house is out of order, they seem to be concerned about "what is in it for them or "their" ministry, and the fruit of what they teach generally keeps people either complacent in their slumbering (false grace), or motivated to help said teacher grow their own ministry. They do signs and wonders. They deliver people from demons. They prophesy. People line up to get prayed for by them, but inside they are all about themselves.

Matthew 7:15-23 "Beware of false prophets, who come to you in sheep's clothing, but inwardly they are ravenous wolves. 16 You will know them by their fruits. Do men gather grapes from thornbushes or figs from thistles? 17 Even so, every good tree bears good fruit, but a bad tree bears bad fruit. 18 A good tree cannot bear bad fruit, nor can a bad tree bear good fruit. 19 Every tree that does not bear good fruit is cut down and thrown into the fire. 20 Therefore by their fruits you will know them. 21 "Not everyone who says to Me, 'Lord, Lord,' shall enter the kingdom of heaven, but he who does the will of My Father in heaven. 22 Many will say to Me in that day, 'Lord, Lord, have we not prophesied in Your name, cast out demons in Your name, and done many wonders in Your name?' 23 And then I will declare to them, 'I never knew you; depart from Me, you who practice lawlessness!'

Third, the truth of the day will expose the tares and the wheat for what they really are. Jesus said the tares would be removed first. How do you reconcile that with a pre-trib rapture? When did Jesus say he would gather up the wheat and burn the tares? The wheat is here to stay because Jesus is coming to stay! That means you need to be ready to endure the time of the maturity, not so you are ready to die, or ready to get raptured, neither of these need your readiness, but to be ready to bring in the harvest in victory. This requires a certain way of living, and an understanding of Jesus' Plan, called wisdom!

This is what Daniel was told:

Daniel 12:1-3 "At that time Michael shall stand up, The great prince who stands watch over the sons of your people; And there shall be a time of trouble, Such as never was since there was a nation, Even to that time. And at that time your people shall be delivered, Every one who is found written in the book. 2 And many of those who sleep in the dust of the earth shall awake, Some to everlasting life, Some to shame and everlasting contempt. 3 Those who are wise shall shine Like the brightness of the firmament, And those who turn many to righteousness Like the stars forever and ever.

Jesus KNEW his church was going to need wisdom to safely navigate these intensely negative events. Jesus saw the "many who needed turning" to righteousness. He knew many in the Church would need to get a right perspective to lead the many. He saw the Church in our day, and just like we see, He knew it would need correction.

In order to correct the end time Church, Jesus picked out seven churches in John's day that were representative of what His Bride would look like at the harvest. What He told them has matured into OUR day. We are supposed to understand the strengths and weakness of these seven Churches and apply them to our own hearts, families, churches, and cities. There is much coming that must be overcome. There are many rewards for overcoming. Overcoming what, Tom? The Tribulation, of course!

The Book of Revelation is primarily the story of the wedding. After we meet the Groom in Chapter 1, the fiancé in Chapters 2 and 3, and the Father who will preside over the wedding in Chapters 4 and 5, we are whisked right into the Tribulation events. Tribulation is what comes after Jesus addresses His beloved, yet spotty, Bride-to-be. It is the Tribulation that will refine her with fire. Seven spotty, impure, and divided churches go into tribulation, and at the end, out comes one pure and spotless Bride. Once the Tribulation starts, you never hear the word "church" again in Revelation, only saints and the Bride. That is because the promised Tribulation will produce purity spotlessness:

Daniel 12:9-10 And he said, "Go your way, Daniel, for the words are closed up and sealed till the time of the end. 10 Many shall be purified, made white, and refined, but the wicked shall do wickedly; and none of the wicked shall understand, but the wise shall understand.

For the next seven chapters, we will examine each Church and see what the Spirit is saying to the Bride in our hour:

Revelation 2:7 "He who has an ear, let him hear what the Spirit says to the churches. To him who overcomes I will give to eat from the tree of life, which is in the midst of the Paradise of God."

Chapter 2 – Ephesus

"Lacking Love"

Revelation is PRIMARILY the story of a wedding. When we think of Jesus marrying His Bride, we want to get the boy-girl connotations out of the way. We got the idea of marriage from God, not the other way around. Marriage, according to the Bible, is about a legal covenant relationship where two people become one. The wedding in Revelation is about relationship, family position, and inheritance...not about sex or physical attraction. Jesus' Bride is going to become sons and daughters of the most High God of all creation. That means WE are going to share in Jesus' family position and family inheritance. The Father loves us like He loves Jesus. For us to come into a living understanding of that, some things must happen, and the process of those things happening is described in Revelation. Revelation is describing the Father's answer to Jesus' prayer in John 17:

John 17:20-23 "I do not pray for these alone, but also for those who will believe in Me through their word; 21 that they all may be one, as You, Father, are in Me, and I in You; that they also may be one in Us, that the world may believe that You sent Me. 22 And the glory which You gave Me I have given them, that they may be one just as We are one: 23 I in them, and You in Me; that they may be made perfect in one, and that the world may know that You have sent Me, and have loved them as You have loved Me.

For the Bride to be legally united as "one" to God's family, we need to go from being divided and lacking much of the glory of Jesus, to united and walking in a measure of glory that reflects Jesus' glory, the light of His presence, to the world. Revelation is describing HOW this will happen. Once you have a paradigm for that, the Revelation of Jesus Christ quickly becomes one of the most thrilling books of the Bible.

Revelation is also describing the moment the crop of wheat that Jesus planted in Acts 1 enters the point where it is mature enough to harvest. So, Revelation is describing a "harvest season wedding." The wheat and the tares are both mature at the time of the wedding. Many wonder where the earth is heading. Will the earth be righteous or evil at the time of the end? The answer is "yes." It will be the fullness of both. Jesus' Bride needs to be prepared for this reality. The unity and glory is thrilling. But, the truth is, unity happens through a cleaning process. It is "unity by division." Because the process is producing a harvest wedding, Jesus' Bride is sifted...shaken...through a time that the whole earth is shaken. Only TRUE grains, those wholehearted, equally interested, and equally yoked in love to Jesus, who gave it all for the marriage, will get married.

Amos 9:9-12 "For I will give the command and will shake Israel along with the other nations as grain is shaken in a sieve, yet not one true kernel will be lost. 10 But all the sinners will die by the sword—all those who say, 'Nothing bad will happen to us.' 11 "In that day I will restore the fallen house of David. I will repair its damaged walls. From the ruins I will rebuild it and restore its former glory. 12 And Israel will possess what is left of Edom and all the nations I have called to be Mine. " The LORD has spoken, and He will do these things.

This sifting is an intense process. If you do not understand what Jesus is doing, and why He is doing it, you run a high risk of being offended, just like John the Baptist's disciples were offended by what God allowed to happen to John. John's disciples couldn't understand, if Jesus was really the Messiah on earth, why was so much bad stuff happening to the guy who prepared the way. John said "go ask Him yourself":

Matthew 11:2-6 And when John had heard in prison about the works of Christ, he sent two of his disciples 3 and said to Him, "Are You the Coming One, or do we look for another?" 4 Jesus answered and said to them, "Go and tell John the things which you hear and see: 5 The blind see and the lame walk; the lepers are cleansed and the deaf hear; the dead are raised up and the poor have the gospel preached to them. 6 And blessed is he who is not offended because of Me."

God's ways are not our ways. Right now, the Bride is mostly confused about what her Groom is doing, but that is not ok with Jesus. Worthless shepherds have neglected to lead the sheep to the wedding. The truth is, for the last 2,000 years, the Bride was supposed to be entirely focused on the wedding. We are all heading to a wedding. If you are a shepherd, you should be leading the sheep to where the owner wants them. The Bible is clear the owner is taking all the willing sheep to the wedding. We really need to be leading the way to the wedding. All the sheep need to get ready to get married.

If you aren't ready to get married, you aren't getting married. Did you hear that? Those aren't my words, they are Jesus'. Just because no one is talking about this doesn't mean it isn't in the Bible. Check your Bible. Look what it says here:

Matthew 22:2-14 "The kingdom of heaven is like a certain king who arranged a marriage for his son, 3 and sent out his servants to call those who were invited to the wedding; and they were not willing to come. 4 Again, he sent out other servants, saying, 'Tell those who are invited, "See, I have prepared my dinner; my oxen and fatted cattle are killed, and all things are ready. Come to the wedding." ' 5 But they made light of it and went their ways, one to his own farm, another to his business. 6 And the rest seized his servants, treated them spitefully, and killed them. 7 But when the king heard about it, he was furious. And he sent out his armies, destroyed those murderers, and burned up their city. 8 Then he said to his servants, 'The wedding is ready, but those who were invited were not worthy. 9 Therefore go into the highways, and as many as you find, invite to the wedding.' 10 So those servants went out into the highways and gathered together all whom they found, both bad and good. And the wedding hall was filled with guests. 11 "But when the king came in to see the guests, he saw a man there who did not have on a wedding garment. 12 So he said to him, 'Friend, how did you come in here without a wedding garment?' And he was speechless. 13 Then the king said to the servants, 'Bind him hand and foot, take him away, and cast him into outer darkness; there will be weeping and gnashing of teeth.' 14 "For many are called, but few are chosen."

We are living in the time this reality is nearly mature. Right now, a few messengers have been sent out. They have been told of the wedding plans. They have heard from the Father that the harvest is ready, both the wheat and the tares, by the signs of the earth they have confirmed it in the Word. But, many do not want the Book of Revelation to unfold just yet. To not want the events of Revelation to unfold is to not want Jesus to return! This is a very bad state of mind to be in. Maybe You are scared? Ok, Jesus can work with that. Just tell Him. He will help you see you have nothing to fear, but fear itself.

Fear is what will cause the offense that causes the falling away. Perfect love casts out all fear. If you are afraid of the return of Jesus it is simply an indicator that you don't yet grasp His perfect love. Growing deeper in His love by understanding His perfect plans born out of His perfect love is the answer to your fear. Comforting yourself with worldly distractions, even those you might find at church, is only going to increase your fear when the intense things you fear ACTUALLY happen. If you look at the news, they are already happening. You really need to go deep in the intense love of Jesus by getting an understanding of what He is doing, what He expects His Bride to do, and then beginning to uncover all the amazing and beautiful promises that the Book of

Revelation contains. You have to deal with the intense stuff to get eyes to see the good stuff, because both are written in the book side by side, but the enemy is trying to drive many in fear away from the promises. I say "fear go now, in the name of Jesus!"

The Revelation of Jesus Christ (that is the official name, not the revelation of satan or the antichrist, but the Revelation of Jesus Christ) reads like a wedding program. In Chapter 1, we meet the Groom. There are 30 descriptions of the Groom packed into about a page and a half of text. This is the most concentrated truth of the identity of Jesus in the Bible. This is the Jesus you want to know going into the events of Revelation. Like Misty Edwards sings: "He's not a baby in a manger anymore, He's not a broken man on a cross. He's alive, and He's not staying in heaven forever!" Chapter one is the Groom's Chamber. Spend some time there. Our King is amazing. His best friend, John, passed out when He saw for the first time who He was really running with.

Revelation 1:17-18 And when I saw Him, I fell at His feet as dead. But He laid His right hand on me, saying to me, "Do not be afraid; I am the First and the Last. 18 I am He who lives, and was dead, and behold, I am alive forevermore. Amen. And I have the keys of Hades and of Death.

Jesus is entirely in control of what will transpire during the events of Revelation, the events leading up to the wedding. He's got this. But, for love, He refuses to make His Bride-to-Be get ready. If she wants to ignore what is happening, it simply indicates she is more about herself than she is about Him.

Can you imagine? Picture yourself as Jesus, or picture your own wedding just before that last week leading up to it starts...

You are so excited about your wedding. You've made tons of plans. There are places to be, photos to take, and dinners to enjoy, and so much excitement as two lives are about to be joined together, but your spouse to be is really acting like all this is a big chore. He or she intentionally misses appointments because every time they go to one it reminds them that bachelorhood is about to end. He complains about the complicated steps of the wedding. He throws up his hands every time you try and talk about how it will all happen, saying it is too complicated..."I'll just figure it out as I go."

You have taken great pains to arrange what you are going to wear. It will look so good with the flowers on the tables and groomsmen and bridesmaids, but your spouse just figures "hey, someone will just pick me up and take me when it is time, who cares what I look like?" YOU care what he or she looks like! He won't even try to listen to what you are saying for more than five minutes.

But, you have made the plans REALLY clear. You want your spouse excited with you! You are so excited by the arrangements, yet your spouse-to-be won't even take the time to sort out the most important event in both your lives, but also in the life of your Father who has taken so much trouble to plan and pay for the wedding...This is a great offense to the entire family. You must get ready if you really love God. This is what Jesus is saying:

"Why did you say yes if you didn't really want to get married?"

If you live in the hour of the wedding, it should be what your life is about. Many claim "the wedding is at hand," but then do almost nothing to get revved up for the event. How sad this is for the lovesick Groom who is still ravished by His Bride! Jesus will only marry an "equally yoked" Bride. He is only going to marry a Bride zealous in love, because that is how He is.

A lack of lovesickness is the problem the world is facing. There is a reason Ephesus was chosen as the first of the seven churches to be addressed. Loving God with all our heart, soul, mind, and strength is the greatest commandment for a reason, and Ephesus missed that message. Let's look at what Jesus told them:

Revelation 2:1-7 "To the angel of the church of Ephesus write, 'These things says He who holds the seven stars in His right hand, who walks in the midst of the seven golden lampstands: 2 "I know your works, your labor, your patience, and that you cannot bear those who are evil. And you have tested those who say they are apostles and are not, and have found them liars; 3 and you have persevered and have patience, and have labored for My name's sake and have not become weary. 4 Nevertheless I have this against you, that you have left your first love. 5 Remember therefore from where you have fallen; repent and do the first works, or else I will come to you quickly and remove your lampstand from its place—unless you repent. 6 But this you have, that you hate the deeds of the Nicolaitans, which I also hate. 7 "He who has an ear, let him hear what the Spirit says to the churches. To him who overcomes I will give to eat from the tree of life, which is in the midst of the Paradise of God." '

For each of the seven churches addressed in Revelation 2 and 3 there is a pattern to the way Jesus talks to them. Jesus follows the same pattern for each Church. Let's look at this pattern for Ephesus:

1. Jesus addresses the church as the standard of what He is admonishing them to do. Here, for Ephesus, Jesus addresses the church as the one who "holds the seven stars in His hand" and "walks among the lampstand."

(side note: This is symbolic language, but it is entirely "decoded" just a couple of paragraphs before this letter in Revelation 1. The problem most people have with understanding Revelation is that over the years, many have made Revelation a mostly symbolic book. Revelation is NOT mostly symbolic. There are seven main symbols in Revelation and all of them are CLEARLY decoded in the Bible itself. The Bible says when it is symbolic or parabolic. Otherwise, we are supposed to understand it literally. If you take Revelation literally, it is EXTREMELY intense. This is intentional. The events coming ARE extremely intense. Many symbolize Revelation to tone down the intensity. This is offensive to God, because He is interested in getting His beloved Bride READY to meet the intensity. Not hiding from it to be offended later.)

The seven stars are the human messengers to the end time Church. The lampstands are the churches. Jesus is saying "I hold you and walk among you always." He is saying I love you and want to be close to you. Love is what He is correcting the church about. For the next six churches, we will see Jesus always opens by identifying Himself as the shepherd who has gone before them in the exact thing He wants them to overcome.

2. Jesus then encourages the church by highlighting the strength of their walk. Jesus is not the accuser. He is the opposite. He is wonderful counselor. He has all the information and authority to evaluate the Bride, and He loves her. He isn't just waiting for a chance to strike Her down. He says that Ephesus walks in great strength: they do the stuff of caring for the lowly and poor, they are patient, and they are loyal to Jesus and do not tolerate evil, but address it. They hold those who claim to be apostles accountable to the Word. They persevere. Jesus is describing a very disciplined people. They have a ton of integrity that comes from their commitment to Jesus. This is good. But, it isn't enough. Human strength and discipline will not pass through the fire of the Tribulation. Period. It will take a miracle to make it through the Tribulation, on purpose. This is part of the design.

3.   Next, Jesus tells them what they lack. This is to help them overcome the Tribulation. Jesus highlights the thing that will cause them to fall away if they do not repent, which means agree with God, in humility. Jesus is saying discipline will not carry you through the hour that is before you. Your commitment to God will not be enough to sustain you as persecution increases, just like it wasn't enough for Peter when He denied Jesus. What Ephesus is confused about is that in pride, they have placed more weight on the strength of their love for Jesus than His love for them. This is the same error that led to Peter's denial of Jesus. It takes God to love God. There is no love apart from the love that God sends out into creation from His throne.

1 John 4:19-20 We love Him because He first loved us. 20 If someone says, "I love God," and hates his brother, he is a liar; for he who does not love his brother whom he has seen, how can he love God whom he has not seen?

Remember, Revelation is describing the fulfillment of Jesus' prayer in John 17. Unity and glory are going to be the end result. This is impossible without God-centered, God-originated, love. Because love is a fruit of the Spirit, an increase of love expressed can only come from an increasing experience of God's love.

Jesus is telling Ephesus that they are on the wrong track. If they keep relying on their own discipline, rather than pressing in to drawing near to God in wholehearted love, they will find that as confusion increases in the world, it will be harder and harder to tap into the river of love as many voices claiming to define love call them evil. That is what is going to happen, you know. The people of the earth are going to blaspheme...call evil...those patiently loyal to Jesus. They will say "those Christians care more about Jesus returning than loving and doing good stuff for the suffering people of the earth."

This accusation is blasphemy, because the truth is we can do nothing of ourselves. Works flow out of a growing love relationship with God. Right now, we should be cultivating that process of abiding in worship and intercession (the Tabernacle of David) and from that place, letting works of love flow out. The Tabernacle of David, according to Amos and many other prophets, including Jesus, is the safe place for the true grains.

The Tabernacle of David was David's expression of the two greatest commandments. The Tabernacle was a practical expression of loving God with all of the heart, mind, soul, and strength, and from that flowed a good government, loving neighbors as themselves. Jesus is coming to create a whole new government based on love that will crush the evil governments of earth, those based on man's power. The Tabernacle will actually sing and worship the framework of that new governmental infrastructure onto the earth, building a throne for Jesus, in advance of the return of the Messiah.

If you want to be a part of the new government built on true love, you MUST love God first, people second. Those are the two greatest commandments. That is why Jesus said "tarry in the city for power" before you try to do the great commission. You need to be mostly about love (abiding) if you want to be truly powerful.

Luke 24:49 Behold, I send the Promise of My Father upon you; but tarry in the city of Jerusalem until you are endued with power from on high."

Jesus is calling Ephesus back to that night and day upper room experience that birthed them. This is where the power first came. That was the first bloom of exciting love of partnering with the Groom in His plan to take back the world in love. That was the first rain on the seeds that made them sprout, but one rain does not a harvest make. We need to keep presenting themselves to the river of love, or we will dry up and die.

Jesus, in the middle of correcting Ephesus about love, says they have one thing really working in their favor that will help: "they hate the deeds of the Nicolaitans." According to the early church writings of Ireneaus, the Nicolaitans were followers of Nicolas, who was one of the seven people first ordained as deacons by the apostles. The Nicolaitans led lives of unrestrained indulgence. These were the false grace guys of the early church. They claimed that Jesus paid the price for sin, so there was no longer sin attached to believers. Whatever they did was ok, since Jesus loved them and paid for their mistakes. This is false grace. Jesus doesn't give grace to live outside of His leadership. Jesus gives grace for us to come more and more under His leadership. When we make a mistake, we turn to Jesus confident in His love and repent. We agree with God that sin is sin and we tell Him we disagree with our sin and ask Him to bring us into a closer walk with Him. Grace is given for repentance to take place in confidence, so we won't be trapped in condemnation. Anything less than growing in love, which according to Jesus IS evidenced by obedience, is taking the grace of God in vain:

2 Corinthians 6:1 We then, as workers together with Him also plead with you not to receive the grace of God in vain.

Although the church at Ephesus agrees with Jesus about false grace, they are also missing the true grace which only grows in our hearts as love grows. The love that Jesus is describing must be sought...like David did as the only true place of safety:

Psalms 27:4-6 One thing I have desired of the LORD, That will I seek: That I may dwell in the house of the LORD All the days of my life, To behold the beauty of the LORD, And to inquire in His temple. 5 For in the time of trouble He shall hide me in His pavilion; In the secret place of His tabernacle He shall hide me; He shall set me high upon a rock. 6

And now my head shall be lifted up above my enemies all around me;
Therefore I will offer sacrifices of joy in His tabernacle; I will sing, yes, I
will sing praises to the LORD.

This zealous love to be with God in continual conversation is practically
expressed individually, but also, according to the Bible, corporately in a
geographic region as David's Tabernacle. This provides the community
with safety in a time of trouble. In His letter to Ephesus, Jesus is
partially addressing the individual believer's value of love, but Jesus is
primarily addressing the corporate body regarding their safety in love.
This is an end time reality. Without love, fear will drive you to falling
away. Look at the context of this famous passage:

1 John 4:16-18 And we have known and believed the love that God has
for us. God is love, and he who abides in love abides in God, and God in
him. 17 Love has been perfected among us in this: that we may have
boldness in the day of judgment; because as He is, so are we in this
world. 18 There is no fear in love; but perfect love casts out fear,
because fear involves torment. But he who fears has not been made
perfect in love.

Jesus is warning Ephesus that they are not ready to endure the
Tribulation, because their lack of love will allow fear to increase, which
will cause the church to shrink back in the face of true persecution
which requires boldness. Death is the consequence. Not the physical
death of their bodies, but real death, which is the falling away into a
permanent lake of fire. The antichrist is going to take away, by law, the
strength of Christians, primarily by confiscating their wealth. You will
not be able to buy, sell, work, pay the electricity, drive the car, etc.,
unless you accept the antichrist's high-tech global currency, called "the
Mark of the Beast."

Revelation 13:16-17 He causes all, both small and great, rich and
poor, free and slave, to receive a mark on their right hand or on their

foreheads, (17) and that no one may buy or sell except one who has the mark or the name of the beast, or the number of his name.

Your heart needs to be ready for this reality. Many will accuse you of not loving your kids if you refuse to take the mark. Families will divide over this choice.

This confiscation of the wealth of Christians is already beginning to happen under the new Islamic Caliphate in Iraq and Syria. Christians are being stripped of all their possessions and being driven out of the Islamic State or killed. This is a reality promised to come to the USA. The stakes in this hour are very high. You must be made bold in wholehearted lovesick loyalty to Jesus. This is what drives out fear and protects you from this:

Revelation 14:9-11 Then a third angel followed them, saying with a loud voice, "If anyone worships the beast and his image, and receives his mark on his forehead or on his hand, 10 he himself shall also drink of the wine of the wrath of God, which is poured out full strength into the cup of His indignation. He shall be tormented with fire and brimstone in the presence of the holy angels and in the presence of the Lamb. 11 And the smoke of their torment ascends forever and ever; and they have no rest day or night, who worship the beast and his image, and whoever receives the mark of his name."

Jesus said to Ephesus that they were not ready for this reality. Then He said "if you don't repent, I will remove your lampstand." That means to stop being a true part of the church, the Bride, Jesus' Body. That means "falling away." The consequences of ignoring what the Spirit is saying to the seven churches is HIGH...life or death. In fact, that brings us to the last part of the pattern, the reward for love:

4. Jesus promises a reward for repentance. Taking Jesus seriously, rather than giving in to pride that says "I already love God

enough", will establish the church in boldness, which will cause the church to overcome the Tribulation.

Jesus says "To him who overcomes I will give to eat from the tree of life, which is in the midst of the Paradise of God"

Jesus is promising that if we repent of trusting in our own discipline and pressing in to wholehearted zealous love, not only will we stand in boldness and not fall away...we will enter in to the paradise of God day by day...just like David. That "one thing" desire is also the desire of God's heart: man with God. That makes the night and day seeking of God a guaranteed answered prayer.

Jesus himself is the tree of life and we are supposed to eat from this tree. He called himself this more than once:

John 6:54-58 Whoever eats My flesh and drinks My blood has eternal life, and I will raise him up at the last day. For My flesh is food indeed, and My blood is drink indeed. He who eats My flesh and drinks My blood abides in Me, and I in him. As the living Father sent Me, and I live because of the Father, so he who feeds on Me will live because of Me. This is the bread which came down from heaven—not as your fathers ate the manna, and are dead. He who eats this bread will live forever."

So, according to Jesus, HE is the food that brings eternal life. Jesus wants us to partake of the Tree of Life by being connected to Him like branches are connected to a tree.   A tree or vine feeds it's branches from the inside out.   Jesus said He is the vine and we are the branches:

John 15:4-8 Abide in Me, and I in you. As the branch cannot bear fruit of itself, unless it abides in the vine, neither can you, unless you abide in Me. "I am the vine, you are the branches. He who abides in Me, and I in him, bears much fruit; for without Me you can do nothing. If anyone does not abide in Me, he is cast out as a branch and is withered; and they gather them and throw them into the fire, and they are burned. If you abide in Me, and My words abide in you, you will ask what you desire, and it shall be done for you. By this My Father is glorified, that you bear much fruit; so you will be My disciples.

Jesus is saying again here that He is the Tree of Life. There is no life for anything not abiding in Him. The commitment to the night and day upper room, the end time Tabernacle of David, will bring life in full. Making worship and talking to God your primary strength sets you boldly before the throne of God now, before you die. This is what truly causes LIFE to happen now.

Hebrews 4:16 Let us therefore come boldly to the throne of grace, that we may obtain mercy and find grace to help in time of need.

Let all who love Jesus hear what the Spirit is saying to the Church in this hour.

Chapter 3 - Smyrna

"Persecuted"

In Revelation 2 and 3, Jesus looks at His bride-to-be in our day, and then picks out 7 churches way back in John's day that represent the main identities of the Church in our day. These are what I call the "seven characteristic churches" of Revelation. Five of the seven churches: Ephesus, Pergamos, Thyatira, Sardis, and Laodicea are so out of agreement with Jesus that they risk falling away unless they change. That means, according to Revelation 2 and 3, five-sevenths...seventy one percent... of the Church in the end times is out of agreement with Jesus and risks falling away unless she repents and changes her way of living!

If the Bride-to-be is willing to humble herself, listen to what the Spirit is saying, and repent, Jesus will help her "overcome." Overcome what, Tom?! Overcome the Tribulation, which comes next in the Book of Revelation. This is actually quite straight-forward, but many symbolize Revelation because it is so intense, they assume it must "mean something" other than what it clearly means: great trouble is coming! Jesus wants us to just take the main and plain meaning of His Word and get ready.   To get us ready, Jesus holds up two churches for us to study. There are two churches Jesus does not correct: the first is Smyrna, the church currently being persecuted with theft, murder, and oppression for their belief in Jesus.

***Revelation 2:8-11** "And to the angel of the church in Smyrna write, 'These things says the First and the Last, who was dead, and came to* *life: 9 "I know your works, tribulation, and poverty (but you are rich); and I know the blasphemy of those who say they are Jews and are not, but are a synagogue of Satan. 10 Do not fear any of those things which you are about to suffer. Indeed, the devil is about to throw some of you into prison, that you may be tested, and you will have tribulation ten days. Be faithful until death, and I will give you the crown of life. 11 "He who has an ear, let him hear what the Spirit says to the churches. He who overcomes shall not be hurt by the second death." '*

Jesus states that Smyrna is already undergoing tribulation, but that has given them great wealth. He is talking about true wealth, which endures forever. Smyrna is wealthy in part because they are actually ready for what is coming to the whole globe. In fact, they are the first fruits of the Tribulation. They are enduring the persecution in advance of what will soon envelope the whole globe. There is much we can learn from Smyrna, because what Smyrna is undergoing is going to eventually spread out to the ends of the earth. Trouble is going to all nations. This is one of the most established end time realities in the Bible:

Revelation 3:10 Because you have kept My command to persevere, I also will keep you from the hour of trial which shall come upon the whole world, to test those who dwell on the earth.

Now, to be "kept from" the hour of trial...some translations call this "tribulation," does NOT mean to be raptured. This is actually quite clear in the Bible. The word the Bible uses for "kept" here is "tereo" (Strong's G5083):

From τηρός teros (a *watch*; perhaps akin to G2334); to *guard* (from *loss* or *injury*, properly by keeping *the eye* upon)

This is the exact same word that Jesus uses when praying for His disciples in John 17, and is a very specific promise for the "brotherly love" church that is doing the Key of David:

John 17:15 I do not pray that You should take them out of the world, but that You should keep them from the evil one.

Jesus does not want His Bride taken off the planet in the hour that the Great Commission would finally be completed. The great commission was given to the Bride. Since God does not change, only the Bride can complete the great commission, and she will in great power:

Revelation 7:9-10 After these things I looked, and behold, a great multitude which no one could number, of all nations, tribes, peoples, and tongues, standing before the throne and before the Lamb, clothed with white robes, with palm branches in their hands, 10 and crying out with a loud voice, saying, "Salvation belongs to our God who sits on the throne, and to the Lamb!"

Revelation 7:13-14 Then one of the elders answered, saying to me, "Who are these arrayed in white robes, and where did they come from?" 14 And I said to him, "Sir, you know." So he said to me, "These are the ones who come out of the great tribulation, and washed their robes and made them white in the blood of the Lamb.

The completion of the Great Commission is one of the most significant events explained in Revelation. Revelation is all about SALVATION. People will be getting saved throughout each step of Revelation. Tribulation is really evidence of light coming into the darkness and incrementally destroying evil. As this happens, light will shine brighter and darkness will get deeper. The difference is going to be dramatic on purpose, so that those who really want truth will choose Jesus. Revelation describes Jesus using the least intense means to reach the greatest number of people at the deepest heart level without ever violating the free will of anyone. Because the stain of sin is so dark and deep, the "least intense means" of shining light are still really intense.

This entire process, which includes events extremely offensive to lukewarm Christians, will result in both the betrayal of a large portion of the church that results in falling away (people leaving the true Church), and bringing a huge group that is currently outside of a relationship with Jesus into the Church. All of this happens in the context of TRIBULATION. Tribulation is a necessary part of the process. It is simply evidence that the change coming to earth is real. Jesus warned His disciples to be ready for tribulation, because the transition to the age to come is so real. Tribulation is the evidence of real change. If you aren't ready for the massive change, offense, which leads to betrayal, becomes a very real danger:

Matthew 24:8-14 All these are the beginning of sorrows. 9 "Then they will deliver you up to tribulation and kill you, and you will be hated by all nations for My name's sake. 10 And then many will be offended, will betray one another, and will hate one another. 11 Then many false prophets will rise up and deceive many. 12 And because lawlessness will abound, the love of many will grow cold. 13 But he who endures to the end shall be saved. 14 And this gospel of the kingdom will be preached in all the world as a witness to all the nations, and then the end will come.

The Tribulation hits the Church first. The change happens from the inside out. Judgment starts in the house of God, because the Bride is supposed to be most ready:

1 Peter 4:16-17 Yet if anyone suffers as a Christian, let him not be ashamed, but let him glorify God in this matter. 17 For the time has come for judgment to begin at the house of God; and if it begins with us first, what will be the end of those who do not obey the gospel of God?

Judgment is the same as tribulation. It is the sifting process at the time of the harvest. Back in the day, before we had big machines to process grain, there was a threshing process that separated the grain from all the stuff that wasn't grain, called chaff. Sifting, or "threshing," was the harvest act of shaking the grain and tossing it up into the wind to see what got blown off. Jesus is going to do the same thing in the final years leading up to His return. He is causing the wind and the shaking. The true grain will remain on earth and establish His reign over all in partnership with Him. The chaff is going to be burned up. You really want to be ready for this sifting process, because the sifting is necessary for Jesus to eliminate the parts of His body that are not true grains:

Amos 9:9-10 "For surely I will command, And will sift the house of Israel among all nations, As grain is sifted in a sieve; Yet not the smallest grain shall fall to the ground. 10 All the sinners of My people shall die by the sword, Who say, 'The calamity shall not overtake nor confront us.'

This sifting, or threshing, process all happens in relationship to what happens in Israel, according to Amos and many others.

The whole earth is "Israel-centric." This is a very important thing to understand in our hour of history. If you haven't turned on the news in the last six months, Israel is on fire and so are the Middle Eastern nations surrounding it. Unlike Las Vegas, what happens in Israel and the Middle East does not stay in Israel or the Middle East, it always spreads out over the earth. Earth was created this way.

God put Adam and Eve in the Garden of Eden and told them to spread out from there having dominion over the earth:

Genesis 1:28 Then God blessed them, and God said to them, "Be fruitful and multiply; fill the earth and subdue it; have dominion over the fish of the sea, over the birds of the air, and over every living thing that moves on the earth."

Where did God put man to start this dominion? The Middle East!:

Genesis 2:10-15 Now a river went out of Eden to water the garden, and from there it parted and became four riverheads. 11 The name of the first is Pishon; it is the one which skirts the whole land of Havilah, where there is gold. 12 And the gold of that land is good. Bdellium and the onyx stone are there. 13 The name of the second river is Gihon; it is the one which goes around the whole land of Cush. 14 The name of the third river is Hiddekel; it is the one which goes toward the east of Assyria. The fourth river is the Euphrates. 15 Then the LORD God took the man and put him in the garden of Eden to tend and keep it.

Mankind was supposed to extend God's government over the new earth from the middle. Sin came into the garden and extended over the whole earth starting in the Middle East. When Jesus came and paid the price for sin, He came to the Middle East, and salvation went out from Jerusalem to the ends of the earth:

Luke 24:46-49 Then He said to them, "Thus it is written, and thus it was necessary for the Christ to suffer and to rise from the dead the third day, 47 and that repentance and remission of sins should be preached in His name to all nations, beginning at Jerusalem. 48 And you are witnesses of these things. 49 Behold, I send the Promise of My Father upon you; but tarry in the city of Jerusalem until you are endued with power from on high."

Acts 1:8 But you shall receive power when the Holy Spirit has come upon you; and you shall be witnesses to Me in Jerusalem, and in all Judea and Samaria, and to the end of the earth."

This is how the world works. What starts in Jerusalem goes out, like a ripple from a stone hitting a pond, to the ends of the earth. The stuff you see in Jerusalem and the surrounding countries right now is promised to touch the ends of the earth. Whatever you see in Jerusalem will happen around the globe in the same way, but to a lesser degree...both the good stuff and the bad stuff. The greatest revival will come to Jerusalem in the end time, but great revival will also touch the Church across the earth. Likewise, the Great Tribulation will be the worst in Jerusalem:

Zechariah 14:1-2 Behold, the day of the LORD is coming, And your spoil will be divided in your midst. 2 For I will gather all the nations to battle against Jerusalem; The city shall be taken, The houses rifled, And the women ravished. Half of the city shall go into captivity, But the remnant of the people shall not be cut off from the city.

But the same thing will touch every nation of the earth:

Isaiah 24:1-13 Look! The LORD is about to destroy the earth and make it a vast wasteland. He devastates the surface of the earth and scatters the people. 2 Priests and laypeople, servants and masters, maids and mistresses, buyers and sellers, lenders and borrowers, bankers and debtors—none will be spared. 3 The earth will be completely emptied and looted. The LORD has spoken! 4 The earth mourns and dries up, and the crops waste away and wither. Even the greatest people on earth waste away. 5 The earth suffers for the sins of its people, for they have twisted God's instructions, violated His laws, and broken His everlasting covenant. 6 Therefore, a curse consumes the earth. Its people must pay the price for their sin. They are destroyed by fire, and only a few are left alive. 7 The grapevines waste away, and there is no new wine. All the merrymakers sigh and mourn. 8 The cheerful sound of tambourines is stilled; the happy cries of celebration are heard no more. The melodious chords of the harp are silent. 9 Gone are the joys of wine and song; alcoholic drink turns bitter in the mouth. 10 The city writhes in chaos; every home is locked to keep out intruders. 11 Mobs gather in the streets, crying out for wine. Joy has turned to gloom. Gladness has been banished from the land. 12 The city is left in ruins, its gates battered down. 13 Throughout the earth the story is the same—only a remnant is left, like the stray olives left on the tree or the few grapes left on the vine after harvest.

This is clear in the Bible, and friends, although few teachers seem to be talking about this, the signs of the times clearly indicate this is unfolding before our very eyes. This is an offensive message. I don't warn of this to make new friends. I had more friends and a better reputation before I fell into this blessing of seeing the time. In fact, this message has cost me some friendships and gotten me a little ridicule. But it has made me one of the best friends of Jesus. He promised His friends to expect that THIS message would offend people who had their own plans for their time on earth, but would please God greatly:

Luke 21:12-17 "But before all this occurs, there will be a time of great persecution. You will be dragged into synagogues and prisons, and you will stand trial before kings and governors because you are My followers. 13 But this will be your opportunity to tell them about Me. 14 So don't worry in advance about how to answer the charges against you, 15 for I will give you the right words and such wisdom that none of your opponents will be able to reply or refute you! 16 Even those closest to you—your parents, brothers, relatives, and friends—will betray you. They will even kill some of you. 17 And everyone will hate you because you are My followers.

I have been called before more than one board of people for the specific way I simply declare the truth: that what is happing in the Middle East is a HUGE indicator of what is rushing toward the rest of the world like a freight train. According to Jesus, it is contending for this truth that gets you brought before the church boards first, and later the government forces. The Bible is clear that tribulation is coming to America, and by the signs of the times, it is coming soon. This requires advanced preparation to deal with it well and not fall away. That brings us back to Smyrna.

Jesus held up Smyrna as one of two churches that were ready for the Tribulation. There are two ways to get ready for the Tribulation: One, the Philadelphia way (night and day prayer as a community that opens heaven and protects the community from Great Tribulation); and two, The Smyrna "experience" (getting a paradigm to endure persecution no matter the personal cost).

Both of these ways are about dying. Both churches learned to die to themselves in advance of people wanting to kill them. Philadelphia did it by trading the "good life" for complete commitment to night and day prayer like David (we'll talk about that in depth later) they were ruined for the world by tapping into heaven as their main occupation, like David.

Smyrna was located in a place that choosing Jesus was the same as choosing death! They picked Jesus knowing it would kill them. Thus, they were already prepared to endure the Tribulation without giving into offense and falling away. You cannot kill what is already dead. If you die to yourself now...for real...you will stand in great victory when the antichrist threatens you with death if you don't give in to his "brilliant" plan to make the earth "fair," by his definition.

Let's break down the fourfold pattern for Smyrna by first looking at how Jesus addresses her:

1. Jesus addresses Smyrna as "the First and the Last, who was dead, and came to life." This is all about the fear of death, and being confident that Jesus knows exactly what it means to conquer death. Jesus is assuring Smyrna they have chosen well,

by choosing Him despite the threat of death. True death is not the death of your physical body, but rather trying to live forever apart from the source of life, which is God. God is WAY more concerned that we don't deny Jesus and suffer permanent death, than that we stay faithful to Jesus and suffer the death of our physical body.

Most of the Church is unprepared for this reality. We imagine that in a split second decision, with a gun to our head, we would not deny Jesus. This may be true, but the reality is that this is not what the antichrist will mostly threaten. Mostly, it will be the ongoing threat of death, the confiscation of all your wealth, imprisonment, threats against your family, the ruination of your kid's future like college or marriage, that the antichrist will use to consolidate loyalty. This requires patient endurance, and strong trust in Jesus' leadership, even though He is invisible. Very real armies will enforce these threats, and it will require a deep commitment to invisible Jesus to endure this patiently. Many, according to Jesus (Matthew 24, Mark 13, and Luke 21), will betray Jesus by taking the Mark of the Beast so they can participate in the modern economy, but they will also betray true Christians to the government for arrest in order to save their own skin.

In the totalitarian regimes that have risen since the establishment of the Church, there is an observable pattern. That pattern includes the persecution of the true church that is loyal to Jesus, and a compromised church that has traded loyalty to Jesus for government protection. This was true in Nazi Germany, Russia, China, Rome. It is clearly beginning to shake out in the USA right now, in this hour, as many denominations cast off loyalty to Jesus and His Word and are bowing to political correctness.

The government church is a satanic tool used to persecute true Christians and allow a government to still look like they are not violating the free exercise of religion. Those who are afraid of offending people

more than they are afraid of offending God will first persecute the
prophetic messengers in their own church organizations so they can
keep the "chicken littles" from offending regular folks. This is fear of
man. If they don't repent, they will eventually offer those loyal to Jesus
up to government forces to save their own skin. The fear of man drives
the compromising church, not the fear of God.

This is a warning to whole communities. If you don't hold your church
leaders accountable to tell the whole uncomfortable truth when the
events of the day clearly match the prophecies of the Bible, they will
eventually resist you if you plan to stay loyal to Jesus as the end times
unfold. Any church leader more worried about his or her ministry than
they are worried about missing what Jesus is doing, is a compromiser. If
you love them, you must address this. Love speaks truth to authority...it
does not remain silent when injustice occurs. Smyrna understood this.
Look at what Jesus says next:

2.   "I know your works, tribulation, and poverty (but you are rich);
     and *I know* the blasphemy of those who say they are Jews and
     are not, but *are* a synagogue of Satan.

Jesus commends Smyrna for continuing to care for the poor and
suffering despite the Tribulation. This has cost them everything. They
are the poorest in the community because of their loyalty to God, but
God says "yes, you are poor for a minute, but forever you will be
wealthy!" This is important to remember: heaven isn't a communist
utopia. We aren't all going to live forever in the same condition. Some
of us will be great and some of us will be least. In heaven there are
"great" and "least":

*Matthew 19:29-30 And everyone who has given up houses or brothers
or sisters or father or mother or children or property, for My sake, will
receive a hundred times as much in return and will inherit eternal life.*

30 *But many who are the <u>greatest</u> now will be <u>least</u> important then, and those who seem <u>least</u> important now will be the <u>greatest</u> then.*

I have heard more than one ignorant teacher say that Jesus would never hold one person up over another in heaven. These teachers are teaching deceit to the body. This will cost many greatness forever. Jesus will certainly reward every believer based on how well they loved Him. Unlike the world, where power, influence and wealth is mostly determined by who you know, Jesus has given ALL of us the ability to be great in heaven forever. It is the most generous system of wealth distribution that could ever exist and is entirely up to each person. If you want to be great forever all you have to do is stay faithful to teach AND do the truth:

Matthew 5:18-19 For assuredly, I say to you, till heaven and earth pass away, one jot or one tittle will by no means pass from the law till all is fulfilled. 19 Whoever therefore breaks one of the least of these commandments, and teaches men so, shall be called least in the kingdom of heaven; but whoever does and teaches them, he shall be called great in the kingdom of heaven.

If you resist, or help the government resist, a man or woman leading Jesus' Bride into wholehearted love for God by faithful declaring what is clearly coming and warning her how to be ready, you are choosing great loss. If you stand for truth no matter the cost, you are choosing great wealth. It is simple.

If you don't stand yourself in faithfulness when you realize trouble is on the horizon and declare it to the rest of the family, you, too, will suffer great loss. The return of Jesus is not a spectator sport. It requires a response. This is what Jesus was telling Smyrna by calling Himself the first and the last and then connecting the faithfulness of Smyrna to His identity:

Revelation 22:12-13 "And behold, I am coming quickly, and My reward is with Me, to give to every one according to his work. 13 I am the Alpha and the Omega, the Beginning and the End, the First and the Last."

There will be least AND great when Jesus shows up.

Revelation 19:5 Then a voice came from the throne, saying, "Praise our God, all you His servants and those who fear Him, both small and great!"

Many who spent decades laboring in the harvest fields will risk losing their crown because they did not love the day of Jesus appearing, and all the trouble that comes with it. This is the offense Jesus warned of. You must guard your heart against this in advance, or come into repentance if you find yourself not loving the events of His appearing:

Revelation 3:11 Behold, I am coming quickly! Hold fast what you have, that no one may take your crown.

Paul, who wrote a huge portion of the Bible, contended that even HE would not lose his faith and keep his crown, despite the tribulation he endured. It is only arrogance that would tell a man's soul he didn't need to guard against the same loss:

2 Timothy 4:7-8 I have fought the good fight, I have finished the race, I have kept the faith. 8 Finally, there is laid up for me the crown of righteousness, which the Lord, the righteous Judge, will give to me on that Day, and not to me only but also to all who have loved His appearing.

Jesus loves Smyrna's faithfulness. Their experience has already proven they are ready. Let's look at the next thing He tells her:

3. Jesus commends Smyrna to keep doing what they have been doing. They are about to enter into greater trouble, but keeping the same heart posture will endure the trouble:

Revelation 2:10-11 Do not fear any of those things which you are about to suffer. Indeed, the devil is about to throw some of you into prison, that you may be tested, and you will have tribulation ten days. Be faithful until death, and I will give you the crown of life. 11 "He who has an ear, let him hear what the Spirit says to the churches. He who overcomes shall not be hurt by the second death." '

This was a massive prophetic revelation given to Smyrna. Smyrna, at the time Revelation was written, was the oldest of the seven church cities, and was in the middle of the grouping of the seven churches. Age and location are very important to understand when considering why Jesus picked Smyrna. Smyrna represents the "middle." Smyrna was the oldest and most central church, representing the oldest and most central church of our day: the Copts in Egypt, the Syrian Christians, the Christians in Israel, and Iraq.

Jesus was telling Smyrna that she would enter into tribulation earlier than the rest of the churches and endure it longer than the other churches. Every other church was expecting "one week" (seven years) of tribulation, according to the prophecies given to Daniel. Speaking of the end...called the "70th week" of Daniel... Daniel was told by God the antichrist would do this:

Daniel 9:27   Then he shall confirm a covenant with many for one week; But in the middle of the week He shall bring an end to sacrifice and offering. And on the wing of abominations shall be one who makes desolate, Even until the consummation, which is determined, Is poured out on the desolate."

The antichrist will make a seven year peace covenant between Israel and her neighbors by promising to protect Israel...he is promising to be like God to Israel. This is his big mistake. In order to make this peace covenant, the antichrist, who is not from the Middle East, is promised to partner with 10 Middle Eastern countries in order to make the conditions just right to make peace in Israel. Daniel was told this in an earlier vision:

Daniel 7:24-25 The ten horns are ten kings Who shall arise from this kingdom. And another shall rise after them; He shall be different from the first ones, And shall subdue three kings. 25 He shall speak pompous words against the Most High, Shall persecute the saints of the Most High, And shall intend to change times and law. Then the saints shall be given into his hand For a time and times and half a time.

Daniel was told the arrogant, pompous, and lawless "11th horn" would cause regime change in three countries in order to make the conditions right for his plans for Israel.

One country --the USA-- has partnered with Sunni Muslim countries in the Middle East that have historically supported an organization called the Muslim Brotherhood. By partnering with the Muslim Brotherhood, a Sunni Islam organization committed to the establishment of a caliphate, The USA has used an event called the Arab Spring to uproot two other countries leaders: Egypt and Libya. At the time of this writing, it is clear that the USA is working on uprooting the leader of Syria. The has caused great unrest in the Middle East, which has resulted in the establishment of a revival of the Ottoman Empire caliphate in Iraq and Syria, called "ISIS."

Additionally, the USA is now are actively supporting the Palestinian government, also Sunni, which is now a unity government made up of Hamas and The PLO. What has resulted is TRIBULATION for the

Christians in the Middle East. Even this week, Christians are being commanded to leave Mosul Iraq or suffer death by Saturday. All of their possessions have been stripped from the ones who have chosen to leave. Those who are staying are saying that they are unafraid of men who can kill the body but cannot kill the soul.

Think about Smyrna for a moment. Jesus prophesied that Smyrna...the oldest and central church, the one already in a persecuted state, would be caught in the middle of that end time trouble and be given "10 days" tribulation instead of the 7 days --the week-- everyone else was expecting. This meant that Smyrna would have 10 years of tribulation instead of the seven years every other Christian was supposed to be prepared to endure. This is the mercy of God. Change must come to the earth. That means tribulation must come. God promised to let that tribulation begin in the one church that was ready! Jesus told Smyrna she was ready by her history of being in the center of the trouble. Everything flows out of the center.

Location is very important in the end times. Remember, what starts in the Middle East spreads out over the whole earth. We can see this happening right now. What Smyrna already had to endure by simple geography prepared her to enter into tribulation that most of the world is unready for. To choose to be an open Christian in the Middle East is to choose persecution from the moment of salvation. Throughout the Middle East, true Christians must hide their meetings to avoid arrest. Christians are killed throughout the Middle East daily for simply being Christians. To share your faith is illegal throughout the Middle East.

The Arab Spring, which turned three nations tolerant of Christianity (Egypt, Libya, and Syria) into persecutors of Christians, started on December 19, 2010. According to Jesus, if this WAS the prophecy of Smyrna being fulfilled, this persecution would begin spreading out over the whole earth, from the Middle East out. What has happened since

December 2010? A quick check of the news will tell you a lot. But just consider the headline news of the last year at the time of this writing:

1. Boko Haram has begun intense persecution of Christians in Nigeria to the south.
2. The Islamic state is now forcing Christians out of Iraq and Syria to the north.
3. Libya has been overtaken by those loyal to the Islamic Caliphate.
4. Pakistan and Afghanistan are beginning to wrestle with groups loyal to the Caliphate.

Look at this quote from Voice of the Martyrs regarding Ethiopia, a MOSTLY Christian nation:

"Although Ethiopia is a predominantly Christian nation, Christians in Muslim areas often experience mistreatment and discrimination. In March 2011, Muslims burned more than 60 Christian churches and homes after the reported desecration of a Quran."[1]

Antichristian activity is spreading into Europe. CBN is reporting the increase of Christian persecution and anti-Semitism on the rise in Eastern Europe with the burning of churches, crosses, and synagogues.[2] Drug cartels are increasingly targeting Christians in Mexico. Look at this quote from a Voice of Russia report in January of 2014:

"Over 100 million Christians are currently persecuted all over the world. The shocking revelation was published by the human rights organization, Open Doors in its research paper "World Index of Persecution". Topping the ratings for cruelty towards Christians is North Korea, as well as Islamist extremists from Somalia, Syria, Iraq, Afghanistan, Saudi Arabia, the Maldives, Pakistan, Iran and Yemen. 50 countries were rated by the index, but today Christians are even being persecuted in Europe. "[3]

What started in the Middle East, the "Smyrna" of our day, on December 19, 2010, with the beginning of the Arab Spring, is going global in a 'shocking' way according to news outlets. Look for yourself. These facts and stories are EASY to find. Jesus said this is going global. That is why every time Jesus spoke of His return He said "watch", "pray", and "Be Ready." Are you watching? Are you praying like your life depends on it? Are you ready?

Smyrna was ready, because they ALREADY lived in the epicenter of the world. What starts in the Middle East, always spreads out over the earth. What you see there in the news today, IS coming. Smyrna was ready from the start because in Smyrna they were ALREADY suffering simply by choosing Jesus. They knew how to count the cost because to follow Jesus there was to choose persecution. None of the other churches are identified this way. We need to learn from Smyrna by learning to die to ourselves now, while there is still time, and by coming into an understanding of Jesus' end time plans that will guard us against offense.

That brings us to the reward promised Smyrna:

4. Revelation 2:10 Do not fear any of those things which you are about to suffer. Indeed, the devil is about to throw some of you into prison, that you may be tested, and you will have tribulation ten days. Be faithful until death, and I will give you the crown of life.

The reward for endurance unto death is the crown of life. This is the promise of greatness forever, reigning in a high place with the one who offered His own life. Smyrna understood the high value of sharing in Jesus' suffering in order to make a way for others to be saved. To drink Jesus cup and share in His baptism is to choose greatness forever:

Matthew 20:21-23 And He said to her, "What do you wish?" She said to Him, "Grant that these two sons of mine may sit, one on Your right hand and the other on the left, in Your kingdom." (22) But Jesus answered and said, "You do not know what you ask. Are you able to drink the cup that I am about to drink, and be baptized with the baptism that I am baptized with?" They said to Him, "We are able." (23) So He said to them, "You will indeed drink My cup, and be baptized with the baptism that I am baptized with; but to sit on My right hand and on My left is not Mine to give, but it is for those for whom it is prepared by My Father."

Smyrna crowned Jesus as king over everything, including their own lives, and were given assurance of an eternal crown. A place of close cooperation in the unfolding government of the soon-coming king, and a place of greatness forever, is prepared for them by the Father.

He who has an ear, let him hear what the Spirit says to the churches. He who overcomes shall not be hurt by the second death.

Footnotes:

1. *Voice of the Martyrs" 2013 Persecuted Church Global Report" (www.vom.com.au)*

2. *CBN News "Persecution on the Rise for Christians in Eastern Europe, " February 8, 2013 (www.cbn.com)*

3. *Voice of Russia "Christians under threat: over 100 million persecuted all over the world, " January 9, 2014(www.sputniknews.com)*

Chapter 4 - Pergamos

"Compromising"

Revelation 2:12-17 "And to the angel of the church in Pergamos write, 'These things says He who has the sharp two-edged sword: "I know your works, and where you dwell, where Satan's throne is. And you hold fast to My name, and did not deny My faith even in the days in which Antipas was My faithful martyr, who was killed among you, where Satan dwells. But I have a few things against you, because you have there those who hold the doctrine of Balaam, who taught Balak to put a stumbling block before the children of Israel, to eat things sacrificed to idols, and to commit sexual immorality. Thus you also have those who hold the doctrine of the Nicolaitans, which thing I hate. Repent, or else I will come to you quickly and will fight against them with the sword of My mouth. "He who has an ear, let him hear what the Spirit says to the churches. To him who overcomes I will give some of the hidden manna to eat. And I will give him a white stone, and on the stone a new name written which no one knows except him who receives it. "

Everyone gets what they want. This is one of the hardest truths of the Kingdom of God to understand, because it makes possible both great light, but also great darkness. What we "set our eye" on really matters:

Matthew 6:22-23 "The lamp of the body is the eye. If therefore your eye is good, your whole body will be full of light. 23 But if your eye is bad, your whole body will be full of darkness. If therefore the light that is in you is darkness, how great is that darkness!

This important passage in the Sermon on the Mount is talking about how our eye, what we set our gaze on, or what we desire, directs our path and takes us deeper into that thing we are looking at. You go where you are looking. If you are driving and you stare to the right side of the road, your car will begin veering to the right. If you stare straight ahead while mowing your lawn, you will cut in straight lines. If you are distracted, your lines will bob and weave all over the place!

There is a basic principle of life that you go where you are looking. This is true physically, as anyone who has ever mountain-biked on a narrow trail, or spent any time skiing, surely knows--but this is also true spiritually. You become like what you behold:

2 Corinthians 3:18 So all of us who have had that veil removed can see and reflect the glory of the Lord. And the Lord—who is the Spirit— makes us more and more like Him as we are changed into His glorious image.

The compromising church in Pergamos needed to hear this truth. They were full of zeal to obey God and held fast to loyalty to His name, but they had cast off the Word...fidelity to Jesus as He has revealed Himself in the Bible... as a main priority. Instead, Pergamos began listening to "those among them"...leaders...without testing the words of these smooth talkers, full of smart sounding ideas that appeal to men's logic, prophecies, and dreams. If you don't have the Word as your foundation, you are left with man-based logic, prophecies, and dreams. Over and over, the Bible warns against listening to those who cannot connect their words to the Word.

Jeremiah 23:25-28 "I have heard these prophets say, 'Listen to the dream I had from God last night.' And then they proceed to tell lies in My name. 26 How long will this go on? If they are prophets, they are prophets of deceit, inventing everything they say. 27 By telling these false dreams, they are trying to get My people to forget Me, just as their ancestors did by worshiping the idols of Baal. 28 "Let these false prophets tell their dreams, but let My true messengers faithfully proclaim My every word. There is a difference between straw and grain!

There IS a difference, and Jesus is warning Pergamos they better start identifying the difference or they will fall away as a community.

Let's look at the four-fold pattern for Pergamos and see what the Spirit is saying to us in this hour:

1. Jesus addresses Pergamos by saying He is the one who has "the sharp two-edged sword." Here is a little Bible "code" that is easily decoded in the Word. The Bible interprets the Bible. Always. Everything you need to know is in the Bible. So what is the sharp two edged sword?

Ephesians 6:17 Put on salvation as your helmet, and take the sword of the Spirit, which is the word of God.

Hebrews 4:12 For the word of God is alive and powerful. It is sharper than the sharpest two-edged sword, cutting between soul and spirit, between joint and marrow. It exposes our innermost thoughts and desires.

Ok. Clearly Jesus is coming to Pergamos as THE WORD. This is one facet of who He is:

John 1:1 In the beginning the Word already existed. The Word was with God, and the Word was God.

The writer of Hebrews says that the Word discerns our innermost desires. The end times are all about desire, because in the end

everyone gets what they want. That means individually, we can have
the Word, or something less, usually the desires of mankind. This is an
individual warning, but also, as a community of believers in any
geographic region, it is a warning to the church of a city. If you want to
value, as a community, leaders who speak out of their own heart, with
no ability to connect their words to the Word, then you will get the self-
centered desires in their heart manifest in your community. You will
bear the fruit of the vine you abide in (John 15). If you want THE WORD,
you need to value loyalty to THE WORD.

Your Bible is not just a book, it is the heart of the Man who bought you,
written unchangingly on paper. It is the standard...the gauge or
ruler...of truth. Everything Jesus wants you to value is held up as
valuable in His words. Everything Jesus wants you to be warned about
is clear in His Word. Everything He wants you to war against is also
clear in His Word.

In our hour, the Pergamos problem is most clearly seen in the
charismatic church. I am a charismatic. I love the spirit of prophecy. I
want more dreams. I value visions. But, these are also some of the
most dangerous tools of deception in the Body of Christ. Many use the
prophetic to elevate themselves. The Bible warns over and over against
giving dreams, visions, and man-based logic more weight than the main
and plain instructions of the Bible.

According to the Bible, many zealous and on-fire believers are actually
falsely leading Jesus' body because they have no root in abiding in Jesus.
He is the Word. IF you love Jesus, then you love the Bible. It takes both
the Man Jesus, talking to you through His Spirit, and the Word, that IS
also the man, talking to you, to bear fruit. If you don't abide in both of
these, you are in big trouble. As John Wimber once famously said: "if
you have the Word with no Spirit, you'll dry up. If you have the Spirit
and no Word, you'll blow up. If you have the Spirit AND the Word,

you'll grow up." Pergamos has the Spirit, they seriously are lacking the Word.

2.   Jesus says Pergamos has a lot going on. From the outside, let's look at what Pergamos had a reputation for with Jesus...they REALLY were doing this stuff : "I know your works, and where you dwell, where Satan's throne is. And you hold fast to My name, and did not deny My faith even in the days in which Antipas was My faithful martyr, who was killed among you, where Satan dwells."

Works – they fed and clothed the poor, sought the lost, took care of the elderly, works were no problem.

Where they dwelt – they were clearly not afraid of spiritual warfare. They went after the strongholds. They were not afraid of the enemy. They prayed, no doubt, big prayers and believed big things.

Held fast to Jesus' name – they were loyal. Oh, did they LOVE the name of Jesus. They sing it, they shout it, they use the name of Jesus. They are so zealous for Jesus' name they don't shrink back, even when one is killed in their city for loyalty to Jesus. These ones are faithful to stand.

Jesus simply says: THIS IS NOT ENOUGH.

Pergamos is blowing up, despite the forceful prayers and powerful moves of the Spirit. They have the Spirit, they have the works, they have the ZEAL, but no high value on the Word. The dreamers and self-focused prophets among them are taking this on-fire church for a ride into the falling away. Jesus is saying, "if you don't repent, you will find yourself fighting against ME!" This is exactly where the Pharisees and Sadducees found themselves, making more of man-based logic, their faulty interpretation of what God surely "must have meant, " instead of simple abiding in both the living Jesus AND his written Word.

Acts 5:38-39 "So my advice is, leave these men alone. Let them go. If they are planning and doing these things merely on their own, it will soon be overthrown. 39 But if it is from God, you will not be able to overthrow them. You may even find yourselves fighting against God!"

Jesus connects the compromise in Pergamos to the amazing story of Balaam in the book of Numbers. Balaam was asked to use his dominion, his prophetic gifting, to curse Israel. Balaam knew that his words were only to be an echo of what God in heaven was saying. However, he relied on his own logic and desired to please man more than God. Not knowing God's plan, he left himself vulnerable to actually rebelling against God. God let Balaam have his way, eventually. It is a terrifying thing to have God turn you over to your own desires if they are not also His desire for you. It means great loss:

Numbers 22:10-22 So Balaam said to God, "Balak the son of Zippor, king of Moab, has sent to me, saying, 'Look, a people has come out of Egypt, and they cover the face of the earth. Come now, curse them for me; perhaps I shall be able to overpower them and drive them out.' " And God said to Balaam, "You shall not go with them; you shall not curse the people, for they are blessed." So Balaam rose in the morning and said to the princes of Balak, "Go back to your land, for the Lord has refused to give me permission to go with you." And the princes of Moab rose and went to Balak, and said, "Balaam refuses to come with us." Then Balak again sent princes, more numerous and more honorable than they. And they came to Balaam and said to him, "Thus says Balak the son of Zippor: 'Please let nothing hinder you from coming to me; for I will certainly honor you greatly, and I will do whatever you say to me. Therefore please come, curse this people for me."...

This is where it gets sticky for Balaam. Rather than making God's plan his own plan, Balaam separates from God's desire and basically says "if it weren't for God stopping me, I would go with you...*but* maybe God will change his mind!":

...Then Balaam answered and said to the servants of Balak, "Though Balak were to give me his house full of silver and gold, I could not go beyond the word of the Lord my God, to do less or more. Now therefore, please, you also stay here tonight, that I may know what more the Lord will say to me." ...

God has chosen love, which means God has chosen free will. God honored the desire of Balaam to sell out God for favor with man. It is an awful thing to be given what you want outside of God's plan. Balaam would not love God's plan, which at the time was to bless Israel. Loving God's Word would have spared Balaam much trouble:

...And God came to Balaam at night and said to him, "If the men come to call you, rise and go with them; but only the word which I speak to you—that you shall do." So Balaam rose in the morning, saddled his donkey, and went with the princes of Moab. Then God's anger was aroused because he went, and the Angel of the Lord took His stand in the way as an adversary against him. And he was riding on his donkey, and his two servants were with him....

Now, we get to the part we all remember:

Numbers 22:27-35 And when the donkey saw the Angel of the Lord , she lay down under Balaam; so Balaam's anger was aroused, and he struck the donkey with his staff. Then the Lord opened the mouth of the donkey, and she said to Balaam, "What have I done to you, that you have struck me these three times?" And Balaam said to the donkey, "Because you have abused me. I wish there were a sword in my hand, for now I would kill you!" So the donkey said to Balaam, " Am I not your donkey on which you have ridden, ever since I became yours, to this day? Was I ever disposed to do this to you?" And he said,

"No." Then the Lord opened Balaam's eyes, and he saw the Angel of the Lord standing in the way with His drawn sword in His hand; and he bowed his head and fell flat on his face. And the Angel of the Lord said to him, "Why have you struck your donkey these three times? Behold, I have come out to stand against you, because your way is perverse before Me. The donkey saw Me and turned aside from Me these three times. If she had not turned aside from Me, surely I would also have killed you by now, and let her live." And Balaam said to the Angel of the Lord , "I have sinned, for I did not know You stood in the way against me. Now therefore, if it displeases You, I will turn back." Then the Angel of the Lord said to Balaam, "Go with the men, but only the word that I speak to you, that you shall speak." So Balaam went with the princes of Balak.

Right now, God is in the middle of orchestrating very specific events in the earth. The sheer amount of fulfilled Biblical prophecy regarding the events in Daniel and Revelation over the last 60 years is jaw-dropping, yet many have not studied God's written plan, let alone agreed with Him in the very specific praying required. Repentance is required.

3. Repent, or else I will come to you quickly and will fight against them with the sword of My mouth. "He who has an ear, let him hear what the Spirit says to the churches.

There are many in Jesus' body, right now, in this hour who will tell dream after dream, vision after vision, sermon after sermon, out of their own wisdom and desire. Although they don't intend to, their vision is MOSTLY about their own elevation, because the heart of mankind is slippery and deceitful! They are setting themselves, and their community of believers, up for a fight against JESUS!

Jeremiah 17:9-10 "The human heart is the most deceitful of all things, and desperately wicked. Who really knows how bad it is? 10 But I, the

LORD, search all hearts and examine secret motives. I give all people their due rewards, according to what their actions deserve."

This isn't a warning to someone else. It is a warning to me and to you. Each person must apply this warning to themselves.

It isn't just "pastors" who do this. It is also people who want to be elevated to the pastor's side. Enabling is just as bad as the one being enabled. Fear of man is a strong lure to be flatters and to reward flattery. We must all die to this. If God is your source and your reward, nothing on earth can pull you from victory. If something other than God is your source OR your reward, you are susceptible to manipulation by satan. Satan works primarily through the words of people.

Everyone that hasn't died to themselves is actually in some way or another, looking for a leg up at the cost of Jesus' body! The people want the pastor to notice them, and many pastors want to be elevated by some more important leader. What this results in is the "corporate ladder" in the church. This is the satanic pyramid scheme that has existed for centuries, and what it does is crush most of the people to elevate the few leaders. Every time. This is the tower of Babel in the Church.

What God scattered at Babel is the spirit of the Harlot. The end time apostate church is the "prostitute" trying to do the same thing the Bride is supposed to do. God calls the end time apostate church the Harlot Babylon. The prostitute works for what she gets out of it. The Bride works for love and covenant commitment, which is complete loyalty to the Groom and His leadership. God traces this adultery back to Nimrod and His first global empire.

Nimrod convinced Babel that it was in their best interest to build Him a nice throne on a tower so he could be god AND king to the people. You can't just come right out and say "people, I am so awesome. Why don't

you build me an amazing ministry so I can bless you with my wisdom!"
So instead, you need to cast a vision that puts you in the role you want,
and sell it that way. Rather than tell the people he intended to rule over
them, I believe Nimrod convinced the people to say this:

Genesis 11:4 Then they said, "Come, let's build a great city for
ourselves with a tower that reaches into the sky. This will make us
famous and keep us from being scattered all over the world."

Who was going to sit on the top of that tower? Not "ourselves." History
shows "ourselves" never get the good end of this sort of deal. No, it
was Nimrod! I believe that if you read between the lines you can see
that Nimrod, by casting the vision from His own heart, was really saying
this: "why don't you build a great city for me, so I can rule over you, and
you can make a name for me." No one can come out and say THAT,
even if it is hidden in their heart. Instead, they need a collective group
to create something for them.

The spirit of the fear of man makes people act foolishly. The fool says in
his heart "God is not going to fulfill the desire of my heart unless I help
him a little." Wisdom begins with the fear of the Lord. If you let the
foolish ones who are not trusting God lead you, then you are following a
fool. Psalm 14 warns of this:

Psalms 14:1-7 To the Chief Musician. A Psalm of David. The fool has
said in his heart,"There is no God." They are corrupt, They have done
abominable works, There is none who does good. 2 The LORD looks
down from heaven upon the children of men, To see if there are any
who understand, who seek God. 3 They have all turned aside, They
have together become corrupt; There is none who does good, No, not
one. 4 Have all the workers of iniquity no knowledge, Who eat up my
people as they eat bread, And do not call on the LORD? 5 There they
are in great fear, For God is with the generation of the righteous. 6
You shame the counsel of the poor, But the LORD is his refuge. 7 Oh,

that the salvation of Israel would come out of Zion! When the LORD brings back the captivity of His people, Let Jacob rejoice and Israel be glad.

They have "all together" become corrupt. That is what Jesus is warning Pergamos about. Despite the power of the Spirit moving on them, the weight of what is coming will crush them because they have removed the foundation of the rock. The Word is a rock that will not move. No storm can move it. Lacking complete loyalty to the Word, to the point you search out the brilliant plans of the Groom, leaves you ready to collapse in a time of judgment. Many will be surprised on that day:

Matthew 7:14-27 Because narrow is the gate and difficult is the way which leads to life, and there are few who find it. 15 "Beware of false prophets, who come to you in sheep's clothing, but inwardly they are ravenous wolves. 16 You will know them by their fruits. Do men gather grapes from thornbushes or figs from thistles? 17 Even so, every good tree bears good fruit, but a bad tree bears bad fruit. 18 A good tree cannot bear bad fruit, nor can a bad tree bear good fruit. 19 Every tree that does not bear good fruit is cut down and thrown into the fire. 20 Therefore by their fruits you will know them. 21 "Not everyone who says to Me, 'Lord, Lord,' shall enter the kingdom of heaven, but he who does the will of My Father in heaven. 22 Many will say to Me in that day, 'Lord, Lord, have we not prophesied in Your name, cast out demons in Your name, and done many wonders in Your name?' 23 And then I will declare to them, 'I never knew you; depart from Me, you who practice lawlessness!' 24 "Therefore whoever hears these sayings of Mine, and does them, I will liken him to a wise man who built his house on the rock: 25 and the rain descended, the floods came, and the winds blew and beat on that house; and it did not fall, for it was founded on the rock. 26 "But everyone who hears these sayings of Mine, and does not do them, will be like a foolish man who built his house on the sand: 27 and the rain descended, the

*floods came, and the winds blew and beat on that house; and it fell.
And great was its fall."*

This is a warning to the Church. If you are in the Church, it is a warning
to you, too. It is arrogance to not think this warning is for you. Jesus
didn't teach stuff we don't need to hear.

Many have "leaderitis." In the Bible, there are NOT two classes of
Christians, yet we have many who believe in "leaders" and "people."
There is ONE body. Every part of the body is a leader in its thing. Only
the esophagus can be the esophagus, and you aren't living' without it.
That makes it just as important as the mouth, though the mouth can
make a lot more noise. A true great one humbles themselves, listens to
others through the filter of the Word, and finds what others are called
to, then helps them become better at leading. The whole body is built
UP this way:

*1 Corinthians 12:20-26 But now indeed there are many members, yet
one body. 21 And the eye cannot say to the hand, "I have no need of
you"; nor again the head to the feet, "I have no need of you." 22 No,
much rather, those members of the body which seem to be weaker are
necessary. 23 And those members of the body which we think to be
less honorable, on these we bestow greater honor; and our
unpresentable parts have greater modesty, 24 but our presentable
parts have no need. But God composed the body, having given greater
honor to that part which lacks it, 25 that there should be no schism in
the body, but that the members should have the same care for one
another. 26 And if one member suffers, all the members suffer with it;
or if one member is honored, all the members rejoice with it.*

Many in Jesus' body enable the dividing of the body by flattering and
rewarding flattery, this creates "leaders" and "people". Everyone needs
to lead in their area. To elevate some over others is really bad for the
leaders and the people.

James 2:1-4 My brethren, do not hold the faith of our Lord Jesus Christ, the Lord of glory, with partiality. 2 For if there should come into your assembly a man with gold rings, in fine apparel, and there should also come in a poor man in filthy clothes, 3 and you pay attention to the one wearing the fine clothes and say to him, "You sit here in a good place," and say to the poor man, "You stand there," or, "Sit here at my footstool," 4 have you not shown partiality among yourselves, and become judges with evil thoughts?

Because the church has not held leaders with microphones accountable to be just like everybody else, and instead want to treat them as special, mostly so the leaders will like them more, they leave the leaders unchecked by the Word. This is not love.

Many "leaders" have started to buy into their own PR. They don't think this is why they like to sit in the front row, gather with the other pastors at events, and be called by some formal name that others don't have, but it often is. If you sit in the front because that is the closest place to where you need to work, awesome. But if you sit in the front everywhere you go because you want to be "that guy," then you have a problem, friend. If the only people you chill with when the "show" starts are the pastors, you have a problem. If you like to hear, "you flow in power," "that was so anointed," or "you really impacted me" from people, rather than hear "well done good and faithful servant" or "you really move MY heart" in secret when it is just you and Jesus, you are in BIG danger. If this is you, it means you love the praises of men and women more than you love the man Christ Jesus and His intense plans clearly unfolding in this hour. A true friend of the bridegroom doesn't flirt with the Bride...that disloyal friend gets beat up when the groom shows up, and rightly so!

It isn't just people that need to use the microphone to lead that have the problem. If you drop a conversation with a friend because someone more important walks in the room, you have "leaderitis," too. If you think that someone "important" has to hear your vision or dream for it to be valid, your heart is sick. If you only have really flattering things to say to "leaders", but can carry on a normal conversation with everybody else, you are dividing the body in a way that will help to compromise loyalty to the Word at some point.

If the community doesn't guard against "leaderitis", it risks falling away from fidelity to the Word, which IS Jesus. Treating certain people this way divides the body into classes and leaves them in perilous danger. Jesus connected this very attitude to the end time judgment that comes with His return:

Matthew 23:1-39 Then Jesus said to the crowds and to His disciples, 2 "The teachers of religious law and the Pharisees are the official interpreters of the law of Moses. 3 So practice and obey whatever they tell you, but don't follow their example. For they don't practice what they teach. 4 They crush people with unbearable religious demands and never lift a finger to ease the burden. 5 "Everything they do is for show. On their arms they wear extra wide prayer boxes with Scripture verses inside, and they wear robes with extra long tassels. 6 And they love to sit at the head table at banquets and in the seats of honor in the synagogues. 7 They love to receive respectful greetings as they walk in the marketplaces, and to be called 'Rabbi.' 8 "Don't let anyone call you 'Rabbi,' for you have only one teacher, and all of you are equal as brothers and sisters. 9 And don't address anyone here on earth as 'Father,' for only God in heaven is your spiritual Father. 10 And don't let anyone call you 'Teacher,' for you have only one teacher, the Messiah. 11 The greatest among you must be a servant. 12 But those who exalt themselves will be humbled, and those who humble themselves will be exalted. 13 "What sorrow awaits you teachers of religious law and you Pharisees. Hypocrites! For you shut the door of the Kingdom of Heaven in people's faces. You won't go in yourselves, and you don't let others enter either...

Elevating "leaders" will always "shut the door" on the true move of God. In its context, this is an end time correction. The fullness of the judgment for this error happens in the generation Israel will invite Jesus back as Messiah...that is our generation.

THAT is why Jesus is correcting Pergamos. That brings us to part 4 of the pattern. The reward for overcoming the Tribulation by repenting NOW, while there is time:

4. Pergamos is not beyond hope. In fact, if Pergamos will repent, two huge rewards are available. "To him who overcomes I will give some of the hidden manna to eat. And I will give him a white stone, and on the stone a new name written which no one knows except him who receives it. " '

The reward for overcoming leaderitis and holding the Word as the standard of Revelation and the rock of the community is that you get MORE OF THE WORD!! Hidden Manna means new hidden revelation...uncommon understanding of the Word! Jesus said the Word is food:

Matthew 4:3-4 Now when the tempter came to Him, he said, "If You are the Son of God, command that these stones become bread." 4 But He answered and said, "It is written, 'MAN SHALL NOT LIVE BY BREAD ALONE, BUT BY EVERY WORD THAT PROCEEDS FROM THE MOUTH OF GOD.'

What is even better, is that the community will get a revelation of their TRUE identity, individually AND corporately. The name that no one else knows on a "white" stone. This is describing a trophy from Jesus with your REAL name on it.

The truth is, Jesus doesn't want you to settle for the evaluation of other people, or the validation of others, because no one has enough information to truly evaluate you or to know how faithful you were to what Jesus told you to do. No one really knows enough about you to give you an identity! To love the Truth is to keep yourself for His evaluation alone. Jesus doesn't want us to give to another what only belongs to Him. Can you imagine if your spouse wanted to know what other people thought of their looks or lives more than you did?! Oh, the pain that would cause you. That would be a violation of the close relationship represented by "two becoming one."

On one day only one opinion will matter. When you see Jesus in His glory, you won't claim any title, you won't pull out your resume, and you won't drop one name. You will most likely fall flat on your face like every other person in the Bible that has seen Jesus. From that moment on, no one else's opinion of you will matter.   You can settle for the name people give you, or you can stay faithful to Jesus and get your REAL reward...an identity that will forever satisfy you! Everyone gets what they want.

He who has an ear, let him hear what the Spirit says to the churches.

Chapter 5 – Thyatira

"Corrupt"

Revelation 2:18-29 "And to the angel of the church in Thyatira write, 'These things says the Son of God, who has eyes like a flame of fire, and His feet like fine brass: 19 "I know your works, love, service, faith, and your patience; and as for your works, the last are more than the first. 20 Nevertheless I have a few things against you, because you allow that woman Jezebel, who calls herself a prophetess, to teach and seduce My servants to commit sexual immorality and eat things sacrificed to idols. 21 And I gave her time to repent of her sexual immorality, and she did not repent. 22 Indeed I will cast her into a sickbed, and those who commit adultery with her into great tribulation, unless they repent of their deeds. 23 I will kill her children with death, and all the churches shall know that I am He who searches the minds and hearts. And I will give to each one of you according to your works. 24 "Now to you I say, and to the rest in Thyatira, as many as do not have this doctrine, who have not known the depths of Satan, as they say, I will put on you no other burden. 25 But hold fast what you have till I come. 26 And he who overcomes, and keeps My works until the end, to him I will give power over the nations— 27 'HE SHALL RULE THEM WITH A ROD OF IRON; THEY SHALL BE DASHED TO PIECES LIKE THE POTTER'S VESSELS'— as I also have received from My Father; 28 and I will give him the morning star. 29 "He who has an ear, let him hear what the Spirit says to the churches."

Jesus sees what is happening in the Church better than anyone else. The Church IS Jesus' body, and He is the great physician. In this hour, Jesus is releasing insight into the seven characteristic end-time churches so that those with humble hearts will see where THEY need correction and repent. For the church in Thyatira, Jesus is telling them that He sees where their loyalty really lies. Corruption has snuck into the church, and many who know better are actually abiding the corruption because of political correctness. They know the Word, what they lack is the fear of the Lord. This is foolishness, what God wants is the fear of the Lord, not for His sake, but for our sake:

Proverbs 14:26-27 In the fear of the LORD there is strong confidence, And His children will have a place of refuge. 27 The fear of the LORD is a fountain of life, To turn one away from the snares of death.

The fear of the Lord is a fountain of life because it is what makes a community of God's people safe! Thyatira feared offending people more than they feared offending God! The church at Thyatira, though they knew something wasn't right in their midst, feared upsetting the leaders who were in error and the people who liked them. Because they are unwilling to rock the boat, those who knew the truth in the church were actually witnessing the falling away of Jesus' body in their midst. Jesus is NOT ok with this! We are supposed to contend for the truth:

Jude 1:3-5 Beloved, while I was very diligent to write to you concerning our common salvation, I found it necessary to write to you exhorting you to contend earnestly for the faith which was once for all delivered to the saints. 4 For certain men have crept in unnoticed, who long ago were marked out for this condemnation, ungodly men, who turn the grace of our God into lewdness and deny the only Lord God and our Lord Jesus Christ. 5 But I want to remind you, though you once knew this, that the Lord, having saved the people out of the land of Egypt, afterward destroyed those who did not believe.

Jude's warning to Church agrees with Jesus' warning to Thyatira: it is not ok to let error go in the church. Letting error go actually reveals the quality of your own loyalty. Those who know the Word and are loyal to Jesus must stand in love and speak truth to authority no matter the personal cost.

This is one of the most pressing issues for the Spirit-filled Church in our day. A quick perusal of the most popular prophecy sites will quickly reveal to anyone who understands Jesus' end time plan that many false prophets are operating in our midst both nationally, and locally. Any prophet or teacher who gives comfort to keep Jesus' leadership at arm's length, teaching the Church that Jesus' highest priority is for people to just "blend in" with the world and somehow the masses will get saved, is watering down the truth of the gospel. Many will fall for this error because it appeals to the flesh. False grace sounds good because it agrees with our natural desires for comfort and popularity that each of us must deal with. We must all deal with the truth of self denial being the main response of accepting the gospel. Many want the gospel without self denial. The problem is, your self is dying...and if you hang onto it, you are dying too.

There is only one gate and one way. Anyone who teaches differently is a false prophet or teacher:

Matthew 7:13-15 "Enter by the narrow gate; for wide is the gate and broad is the way that leads to destruction, and there are many who go in by it. 14 Because narrow is the gate and difficult is the way which leads to life, and there are few who find it. 15 "Beware of false prophets, who come to you in sheep's clothing, but inwardly they are ravenous wolves.

The gate is narrow and the way is hard...on purpose! But many will teach otherwise. They will teach that you can have Jesus and hang on to your life too, like the world gets life! This is a straight up lie, but a very popular one. Who doesn't want all the benefits of Jesus' presence without the narrowness of His leadership? There is only one gospel, and this is the central tenant of Jesus' good news:

Matthew 16:24-26 Then Jesus said to His disciples, "If anyone desires to come after Me, let him deny himself, and take up his cross, and follow Me. 25 For whoever desires to save his life will lose it, but whoever loses his life for My sake will find it. 26 For what profit is it to a man if he gains the whole world, and loses his own soul? Or what will a man give in exchange for his soul?

Anything less than this is a false gospel. There are many false gospels in the world right now. Again, according to Jesus' exam of the end time church, 5 out of 7 of the churches --71 percent-- will fall away if they don't repent and get serious about His return. There is a very specific way disciples of Jesus are supposed to live in the world. We see it most clearly in Acts 5, which is actually the model for the Bride in the end times. The way we are supposed to live is an answer to Jesus' prayer in John 17:

John 17:15-18 I do not pray that You should take them out of the world, but that You should keep them from the evil one. 16 They are not of the world, just as I am not of the world. 17 Sanctify them by Your truth. Your word is truth. 18 As You sent Me into the world, I also have sent them into the world.

Jesus prayed that we would be in the world, but not of it. Living here on earth, but sticking out like a sore thumb, even embarrassingly, because we were so different from the world. That is how Jesus rolled...sanctified...which means "set apart" Jesus loved the world, but He did not act like the world. He was like salt in many wounded hearts. This was designed to SAVE people. Jesus prayed His Bride would be like Him, not taken out of the world, but protected through the persecution that marks everyone living in a way that leaves them sticking out like a sore thumb in a world that is dying because it is chasing after darkness. In fact, persecution for this Jesus lifestyle is the pinnacle of the Beatitudes. The Beatitudes are markers on the trail of the narrow road. When you get to this point in the narrow road, you are breathing rare air, because you are actually the living answer to Jesus' prayer! You are sharing in His life!

Matthew 5:11-13 "Blessed are you when they revile and persecute you, and say all kinds of evil against you falsely for My sake. 12 Rejoice and be exceedingly glad, for great is your reward in heaven, for so they persecuted the prophets who were before you. 13 "You are the salt of the earth; but if the salt loses its flavor, how shall it be seasoned? It is then good for nothing but to be thrown out and trampled underfoot by men.

For a brief moment in Jerusalem, described in Acts 5, the Bride was functioning in unity and holiness, living answers to Jesus' prayer. What resulted was the exaltation of the name of Jesus, because the fear of His name, the fear of the Lord, was touching the whole city. This resulted in the glory of Jesus, the very same power He walked in, being manifest in His reflection in His Bride's face. They healed like He healed, prophesied like He prophesied, cast out demons like He did, and saved the lost like He did. This resulted in persecution, just as Jesus promised, not from unbelievers, but from religious leaders who were desperately trying to hang onto their own jobs as being representatives for God without giving in to God's leadership! Why did those religious leaders take the job in the first place? Because they loved the praises of men. They liked the distinction of being the holy "leaders," not submitted servants. They resisted the Bride that was walking in truth and power because when the world saw truth the Bride, it stopped looking to the old leaders.

In Acts 5 we see that the Bride was so united in agreement with God through the Holy Spirit that lying to the Bride was the same as lying directly to God. Heaven enforced this truth and Ananias and Sapphira found this out the hard way and died on the spot when they lied to Peter and his friends. Peter and the other servants of Jesus contended earnestly by calling out falsehood in the congregation, and God backed them up in power. This demonstration of God's agreement with the Bride released the fear of the Lord in a tangible way both in, and out of, the Church. THIS protected the Church in a very hostile environment, which Jerusalem was at the time. The fear of the Lord became a fountain of life for the early church:

Acts 5:11-16 So great fear came upon all the church and upon all who heard these things. 12 And through the hands of the apostles many signs and wonders were done among the people. And they were all with one accord in Solomon's Porch. 13 Yet none of the rest dared join them, but the people esteemed them highly. 14 And believers were increasingly added to the Lord, multitudes of both men and women, 15 so that they brought the sick out into the streets and laid them on beds and couches, that at least the shadow of Peter passing by might fall on some of them. 16 Also a multitude gathered from the surrounding cities to Jerusalem, bringing sick people and those who were tormented by unclean spirits, and they were all healed.

Thyatira forgot this essential equation. Thyatira's problem, according to Jesus, is that they didn't believe God was more powerful than the people around them, whose opinions they feared. They didn't fear the Lord more than the people claiming to represent Him, and what resulted was the exact opposite of a fountain of life. They were promised death. Instead of building a church that would be protected by the power of God manifest in holiness and unity, they were eroding the foundation of the church by doing nothing as satan attacked from underground. The waves of error were washing away the very rock that would keep them safe in the storm. A storm is coming, and to endure it, you need to contend for holiness:

Matthew 7:21-28 "Not everyone who says to Me, 'Lord, Lord,' shall enter the kingdom of heaven, but he who does the will of My Father in heaven. 22 Many will say to Me in that day, 'Lord, Lord, have we not prophesied in Your name, cast out demons in Your name, and done many wonders in Your name?' 23 And then I will declare to them, 'I never knew you; depart from Me, you who practice lawlessness!' 24 "Therefore whoever hears these sayings of Mine, and does them, I will liken him to a wise man who built his house on the rock: 25 and the rain descended, the floods came, and the winds blew and beat on that house; and it did not fall, for it was founded on the rock. 26 "But everyone who hears these sayings of Mine, and does not do them, will be like a foolish man who built his house on the sand: 27 and the rain descended, the floods came, and the winds blew and beat on that house; and it fell. And great was its fall." 28 And so it was, when Jesus had ended these sayings, that the people were astonished at His teaching,

A STORM IS COMING. If you watch the news and know the Bible at all, you should be able to plainly see the storm is already lashing the shore with waves. Let's look at the four-fold pattern of how Jesus addressed Thyatira to see what WE need to do to batten down the hatches in a way that agrees with God and produces a fountain of life in OUR midst. The antichrist armies will come, but they will not overcome places that live like Acts 5:

1. Jesus addresses the church at Thyatira as the "Son of God, who has eyes like a flame of fire, and His feet like fine brass."

Jesus' "eyes like fire" describe the intensity of His gaze. He both sees everything Thyatira is doing, and desires all of their heart. Jesus desires wholehearted love from Thyatira and He sees the areas that they are compromising. They are thinking "Jezebel is popular, she isn't really hurting anyone with her compromised thoughts, and no one else is saying anything. Who am I to make a big deal about it? Nobody is perfect!" WRONG! Jesus is telling Thyatira HE SEES the compromise, and that compromise will hurt everyone. Feet like burnished brass is describing "feet of fire." This is judgment. Jesus is describing himself as one who judges truth from error. He expects those who see like Him to stand like Him. To not judge what is right or wrong within the fellowship of believers is to actually rebel against God and harm the entire body:

1 Corinthians 5:1-13 It is actually reported that there is sexual immorality among you, and such sexual immorality as is not even named among the Gentiles—that a man has his father's wife! 2 And you are puffed up, and have not rather mourned, that he who has done this deed might be taken away from among you. 3 For I indeed, as absent in body but present in spirit, have already judged (as though I were present) him who has so done this deed. 4 In the name of our Lord Jesus Christ, when you are gathered together, along with my spirit, with the power of our Lord Jesus Christ, 5 deliver such a one to Satan for the destruction of the flesh, that his spirit may be saved in the day of the Lord Jesus. 6 Your glorying is not good. Do you not know that a little leaven leavens the whole lump? 7 Therefore purge out the old leaven, that you may be a new lump, since you truly are unleavened. For indeed Christ, our Passover, was sacrificed for us. 8 Therefore let us keep the feast, not with old leaven, nor with the leaven of malice and wickedness, but with the unleavened bread of sincerity and truth. 9 I wrote to you in my epistle not to keep company with sexually immoral people. 10 Yet I certainly did not mean with the sexually immoral people of this world, or with the covetous, or extortioners, or idolaters, since then you would need to go out of the world. 11 But now I have written to you not to keep company with anyone named a brother, who is sexually immoral, or

covetous, or an idolater, or a reviler, or a drunkard, or an extortioner—
not even to eat with such a person. *12* For what have I to do with
judging those also who are outside? Do you not judge those who are
inside? *13* But those who are outside God judges. Therefore "PUT
AWAY FROM YOURSELVES THE EVIL PERSON."

In Corinth, Paul addresses the same false grace that Thyatira is dealing
with. Rather than address the error before Paul corrected them,
Corinth was celebrating how "free" they were. Their freedom, called
glorying, was actually celebrating the bondage demons were enjoying
by keeping them "politically correct." Only a couple of people were
involved in the obscene sin, but the entire church in Corinth stood
corrected, because they refused to properly address the licentiousness.
Paul said it isn't just sexual sin that is the problem. It is taking the grace
of God in vain in any area, the sexually immoral, or covetous (wanting
the things of the world more than the things of the kingdom), or an
idolater (worshiping life here rather than contending for real life when
Jesus comes back), or a reviler (talking bad about those who are
wholehearted), or a drunkard, or an extortioner (those who trade
power or safety for loyalty to themselves). False grace is the problem,
because it makes those who are salty bland, and the whole lump
becomes good for nothing but increasing corruption in an ever
expanding circle of friends. The difference between Christians and non-
Christians becomes so unnoticeable that no one gets saved and
everyone thinks they ARE saved. This is tragedy when trouble comes.

That brings us to part two of the fourfold pattern. Jesus' loves what they
are doing well

2. *"I know your works, love, service, faith, and your patience; and*
    as for your works, the last are more than the first.

Thyatira looks from the outside like a very successful church. They are
feeding the poor and seeking out the lost. They love Jesus. They

sincerely are in love with the Son of God. They believe in the power of the name of Jesus, they have remarkable faith. They have patience. They are in this for the long haul. They are even growing in doing more and more to impact their city. Jesus loves all these aspects of who Thyatira are. But, He says that this is not enough to make it through the Tribulation. Jesus warns them that if they don't repent, He is sending trouble in advance of the Tribulation to get them to change course. He loves them too much to not judge them:

3. *Nevertheless I have a few things against you, because you allow that woman Jezebel, who calls herself a prophetess, to teach and seduce My servants to commit sexual immorality and eat things sacrificed to idols. 21 And I gave her time to repent of her sexual immorality, and she did not repent. 22 Indeed I will cast her into a sickbed, and those who commit adultery with her into great tribulation, unless they repent of their deeds. 23 I will kill her children with death, and all the churches shall know that I am He who searches the minds and hearts. And I will give to each one of you according to your works.*

This is a very sobering warning. Most of the church at Thyatira did not even subscribe to the false teaching of this one who held herself up as a leader. But, they TOLERATED her, which Jesus says is an error that will lead to the death of many. This was very unpleasing to the Lord.

The amazing patience of God is on display here, because He had given the false prophet much time to repent. The people in the church assumed God must not mind the false teaching too much, because the teacher seemed to stay in power. What Thyatira didn't understand was that the Lord was waiting on THEM to do something about it. He was testing their loyalty to Him, and they were failing big time. Jesus promised that what would result was the death of their own children, who were the most susceptible to false teaching. Jesus said this would be an example to the other churches that His warnings were not just hot air.

Jesus doesn't teach stuff the Church doesn't need to hear. His warnings really matter to keep the Bride in endurance through the Tribulation. There is a judgment for the false teacher, but an even worse judgment for the church that tolerated her. Jezebel would be thrown into sickness, but the church would be vulnerable to the Great Tribulation. If you understand what this means, then you understand how terrifying this judgment is. The Great Tribulation will be the worst time the earth has ever seen:

Matthew 24:15-22 "Therefore when you see the 'ABOMINATION OF DESOLATION,' spoken of by Daniel the prophet, standing in the holy place" (whoever reads, let him understand), 16 "then let those who are in Judea flee to the mountains. 17 Let him who is on the housetop not go down to take anything out of his house. 18 And let him who is in the field not go back to get his clothes. 19 But woe to those who are pregnant and to those who are nursing babies in those days! 20 And pray that your flight may not be in winter or on the Sabbath. 21 For then there will be great tribulation, such as has not been since the beginning of the world until this time, no, nor ever shall be. 22 And unless those days were shortened, no flesh would be saved; but for the elect's sake those days will be shortened.

Sorting out the issues of the seven churches now, while there is time, is essential to be kept safe through the hour of testing which must come upon the whole earth. Only one church, Philadelphia, was held up by Jesus as "safe." If Thyatira will humble herself, repent, and do the hard work of holding her leaders accountable, she will move closer into agreement with Philadelphia and Jesus' prayer in John 17. She will actually begin being the living answer to Jesus' prayer while there is still time for her sanctification to protect her! Remember Acts 5...unity and holiness release power that instills the fear of the Lord IN and OUT OF the Church. This is one of the main ways Jesus will protect the end time Church from the persecution of the antichrist.   To erode holiness is to actually erode safety. Our sanctification doesn't benefit God, it benefits us! Listen to the reward Jesus promises Thyatira if those who know the truth will simply contend for the truth:

4.   *"Now to you I say, and to the rest in Thyatira, as many as do not have this doctrine, who have not known the depths of Satan, as they say, I will put on you no other burden. 25 But hold fast what you have till I come. 26 And he who overcomes, and keeps My works until the end, to him I will give power over the nations— 27 'HE SHALL RULE THEM WITH A ROD OF IRON; THEY SHALL BE DASHED TO PIECES LIKE THE POTTER'S VESSELS'— as I also have received from My Father; 28 and I will give him the morning star.*

The duty of holding leaders accountable is a burden to those who don't agree with Jezebel, they must contend for the truth, but Jesus is saying this is all they lack. If they will choose to fear His opinion more than those who like the "freedom" Jezebel is selling, they will overcome the Tribulation and will have shown themselves faithful to judge not just those in their own fellowship in Thyatira, but the NATIONS...forever.

Those who respond will have shown themselves worthy to be a integral part of Jesus' government over creation forever! They will be the ones sent out to the nations during the millennial reign of Jesus, the 1,000-year "extreme earth makeover" that will return the earth back to the Garden of Eden day by day as the nations are discipled into the saving and living knowledge of Jesus. Overcoming the false prophets in their midst, speaking truth in love, is what will give Thyatira a testimony to overcome sin globally in the age to come. We overcome by the Blood of the Lamb AND the word of our testimony.

Revelation 12:11 And they overcame him by the blood of the Lamb and by the word of their testimony, and they did not love their lives to the death.

The second reward promised to Thyatira for overcoming compromise is even greater. Jesus promises them the "morning star." The morning star IS Jesus, and alludes to His "eyes like fire."

Revelation 22:16 "I, Jesus, have sent My angel to testify to you these things in the churches. I am the Root and the Offspring of David, the Bright and Morning Star."

What Jesus is saying is that if Thyatira will stand like He stands, if they will desire Him more than the approval of the people, He will give them more of Him! He will give them greater eyes of fire, to see more of Him, to know Him more. Everyone gets what they want in the end, and if God's people will put on the fear of the Lord, making His voice the sole voice to obey, what they will find is that His voice will grow stronger and stronger, giving them more and more insight into who He is, what He loves, and how He loves them. This is perfect love that casts out all fear, but He will only give it to those that choose it by casting off every other lover and living faithful and true to the author of love:

1 John 4:17-18 Love has been perfected among us in this: that we may have boldness in the day of judgment; because as He is, so are we in this world. 18 There is no fear in love; but perfect love casts out fear, because fear involves torment. But he who fears has not been made perfect in love.

He who has an ear, let him hear what the Spirit says to the churches.

Chapter 6 – Sardis

"Dead"

*Revelation 3:1-6 "And to the angel of the church in Sardis write,
'These things says He who has the seven Spirits of God and the seven
stars: "I know your works, that you have a name that you are alive,
but you are dead. 2 Be watchful, and strengthen the things which
remain, that are ready to die, for I have not found your works perfect
before God. 3 Remember therefore how you have received and heard;
hold fast and repent. Therefore if you will not watch, I will come upon
you as a thief, and you will not know what hour I will come upon you.
4 You have a few names even in Sardis who have not defiled their
garments; and they shall walk with Me in white, for they are worthy.
5 He who overcomes shall be clothed in white garments, and I will not
blot out his name from the Book of Life; but I will confess his name
before My Father and before His angels. 6 "He who has an ear, let
him hear what the Spirit says to the churches."*

Most of the world does not like process. Because of the fall, impatience
has invaded the space of our hearts where patience once dwelt. The
Sardis church wanted to make a name for herself, and rather than wait
in patience by living in the leadership of the Holy Spirit, which brings life
in abundance, she chose to impatiently "get some stuff going" in her
own strength. Though the world loves what she sells, by relying on her
own logic and marketing, she has actually chosen death, she just
doesn't know it yet. Jesus is warning her that the Day of the Lord, the
process of His return, will reveal just how dead she is:

1 Corinthians 4:5 Therefore judge nothing before the time, until the Lord comes, who will both bring to light the hidden things of darkness and reveal the counsels of the hearts. Then each one's praise will come from God.

Jesus is the source of life, and the Holy Spirit is the connection...the "tether" to Him. The life of Sardis is connected to the operation of the Holy Spirit by Jesus. Sardis, by choosing to care more about her earthly reputation, fearing man's opinion more than God's, has actually shut off the flow of the Spirit, she has severed herself from the vine:

John 15:5-6 "I am the vine, you are the branches. He who abides in Me, and I in him, bears much fruit; for without Me you can do nothing. 6 If anyone does not abide in Me, he is cast out as a branch and is withered; and they gather them and throw them into the fire, and they are burned.

It is by the Spirit that we abide in Jesus. The Holy Spirit is the connection from man to God. He is the "sap" that flows between the Vine and the branch. Letting the sap flow is called living. The more of a connection to God you have, the more abundant life you have. When God made Adam, He formed him from the dust and breathed the Holy Spirit, the Spirit of Life , into Adam through his nostril:

Genesis 2:7 And the LORD God formed man of the dust of the ground, and breathed into his nostrils the breath of life; and man became a living being.

The breath of life IS the Holy Spirit. The word Hebrew "breath" in this passage is n'shamah...which is the "divine spirit of life." God made man to relate to God in love. Love requires a choice to love back, or say "no" to love. Without free will, love cannot exist. So God gave mankind an option to say no to love, for the sake of love!

In God's mercy, He gave Adam and Eve only one choice to say no. If God was looking to disqualify man, he could have only given one option to obey! God was not trying to trick Adam and Eve. In fact, He made the rejection of love a very conscious act, instead of just a rebellious thought. To reject God's love was to choose to take in evil, or the absence of God. Rejection of God's love required a physical act of actually eating the fruit of death, which was a choice to explore life apart from God's loving leadership. Evil isn't an equal and opposite force to God's goodness. Evil is the absence of God, just like dark is the absence of light, and cold is the absence of heat. God is the source, or the light, of life:

John 1:1-4 In the beginning was the Word, and the Word was with God, and the Word was God. 2 He was in the beginning with God. 3 All things were made through Him, and without Him nothing was made that was made. 4 In Him was life, and the life was the light of men.

Adam and Eve knew good, because they knew God. The tree of the knowledge of good and evil was a choice to know the absence of good, which is evil. When Adam and Eve ate the fruit of the knowledge of good and evil, they chose to gaze on darkness. Darkness entered their being for the first time. God is bright holiness, much brighter than the dim sun we are temporarily stuck with. When Adam and Eve ate in darkness, it diminished their infinite capacity to host the bright presence of God in their physical frame. Anything less than infinite is infinitely less. God's light became too much for them. The bright glory of God became deadly to the dark in their being.

God withdrew from the Garden He called "very good" for love, and mankind began the process of dying that day. Although Adam and Eve's physical bodies lived on for a while, the process of death had been initiated by their choice to reject love, which is to reject life.

Mankind was made in God's image –triune-- like the triune God. Man is spirit, soul (mind, will, and emotion, also called our heart), and body. What died that day in the garden was Adam and Eve's spirit, as the Holy Spirit, or "breath of life" exited their frame. Darkness was left in their spirit, which could not live apart from the light of mankind. Shame, which is an awareness of lack, filled the space the Holy Spirit once occupied:

Genesis 3:7-8 At that moment their eyes were opened, and they suddenly felt shame at their nakedness. So they sewed fig leaves together to cover themselves. 8 When the cool evening breezes were blowing, the man and his wife heard the LORD God walking about in the garden. So they hid from the LORD God among the trees.

The spirit of Adam died in the garden, and following close behind, Adam's heart began to die, as the choices mankind made veered further and further from the path God had for man. No longer led by the Spirit of God living on the inside, man was left to the leadership of his soul...his mind, will, and emotions. The sap of the Spirit was no longer flowing. Clearly, life became less abundant. Mankind began to wither. The death of the heart of mankind became more and more apparent as generation passed to generation. Depravity rose up in the hearts of man (their mind, will, and emotion) until the time came where God regretted His creation:

Genesis 6:5-8 The LORD observed the extent of human wickedness on the earth, and He saw that everything they thought or imagined was consistently and totally evil. 6 So the LORD was sorry He had ever made them and put them on the earth. It broke His heart. 7 And the LORD said, "I will wipe this human race I have created from the face of the earth. Yes, and I will destroy every living thing—all the people, the large animals, the small animals that scurry along the ground, and even the birds of the sky. I am sorry I ever made them." 8 But Noah found favor with the LORD.

The initial beauty of salvation is evident in the immediate life brought into the frame of man. Although the heart of mankind is dark and slippery, the presence of the Spirit of God can illuminate the heart and cause it to begin to grow in righteousness again. Shame is what drives mankind to hide from God, but the Holy Spirit put back in the spirit of a man is what draws a man closer and closer to the source of life! The sap begins flowing and life is renewed. Jesus said everyone born again is "born of the Spirit" once again. Choosing Jesus is choosing to have God breathe His Holy Spirit back into your nostrils so you can live led by the Spirit of God once more:

John 3:3-6 Jesus replied, "I tell you the truth, unless you are born again, you cannot see the Kingdom of God." 4 "What do You mean?" exclaimed Nicodemus. "How can an old man go back into his mother's womb and be born again?" 5 Jesus replied, "I assure you, no one can enter the Kingdom of God without being born of water and the Spirit. 6 Humans can reproduce only human life, but the Holy Spirit gives birth to spiritual life.

This is what it means to be "born again": you ask God for life in confidence (faith) that Jesus paid the fare back into life with His unjust death on your behalf. You turn from the dead ways of the world, denying your heart and flesh the leadership they have enjoyed while the Spirit was away, and you commit to learn to let Jesus be the leader of your life through the Spirit inside of you. When you do this, the promise is that the Spirit of life comes back in to your spirit and the process of life begins in you for the first time. If you haven't accepted Jesus on these terms, you are not saved (if you haven't already invited God by declaring this to Him, just go ahead and do that right now out loud if you want to be born again. God is listening. Salvation is as simple as expressing your desire to God to live again on these terms). If you have chosen to live again on these terms, you for sure have the Holy Spirit in you. That means the Genesis 1 Creator God who spoke all of life into being lives on the inside of you. Oh Glory!!:

Ephesians 1:12-14 that we who first trusted in Christ should be to the praise of His glory. 13 In Him you also trusted, after you heard the word of truth, the gospel of your salvation; in whom also, having believed, you were sealed with the Holy Spirit of promise, 14 who is the guarantee of our inheritance until the redemption of the purchased possession, to the praise of His glory.

That means if Jesus is your Savior, then you have the fullness of the Fruit of the Spirit living in your spirit: love, joy, peace, patience, kindness, goodness, gentleness, self control, faithfulness. Just as Adam first died in His spirit, then over time, in a process, his heart died, new birth happens the exact same way. First to come back to life is your spirit, as the Spirit of God takes up residency within you. Many saved people, although their spirit is alive with the very righteousness of God, their mind, will, and emotions (heart or soul) show almost no evidence of it. There is very little love peeking through their choices or thoughts, little patience, little self control, gentleness, or peace.

Because God will never violate love, He will never violate your free will. Just like you need to choose to invite God back into your Spirit, by inviting Him to be the leader of your life again, you must do the same thing with your heart. This happens in a process, just like everything else.

This is how you choose to let the Holy Spirit revive your heart: choice by choice, rather than letting your mind, will, and emotions lead, you deny those things leadership and you draw the leadership of the Spirit into your situation. You do this with your words:

"Holy Spirit, what are you doing in this situation? Why this sickness? Should I take a pill or call on the healing power of the living God within me?"

"Holy Spirit, why this lack? Should I learn to save more money, or to live in the extravagant generosity Jesus taught with the widow and her two mites, giving all she had to live on, so she might live in the smile of God?"

In the weak discipline of our fallen mind, living in the power of God is impossible. But, when we draw on the power of God living within us, the impossible becomes possible, and more and more we are sanctified, or set apart. This is how we need to learn to live to make it through the Tribulation. This is what Jesus prayed for His Bride:

John 17:15-19 I do not pray that You should take them out of the world, but that You should keep them from the evil one. 16 They are not of the world, just as I am not of the world. 17 Sanctify them by Your truth. Your word is truth. 18 As You sent Me into the world, I also have sent them into the world. 19 And for their sakes I sanctify Myself, that they also may be sanctified by the truth.

Jesus is coming back, physically, to planet earth. He is so bright that His coming will literally consume the darkness in the earth. Sanctification prepares you to receive Him in all His glory.

In order to prepare the earth to receive Jesus, God is lifting His restraint from the desires of mankind. Everyone gets what they want in the end, and in our generation, we can clearly see this happening. Evil, the darkness in men's hearts, is going to a whole new level. In this hour evil is increasing because God is lifting his restraining hand from the evil desires in man's heart. In His mercy, for thousands of years, God has, by orchestrating the circumstances of the earth, blocked the full expression of evil in mankind. In the final hours of history before the return of God,

God has promised to lift this restraint and allow everyone to get what they want. This will produce the right conditions for the wheat and the tares to mature. Both evil and righteousness are maturing in this hour. Sanctification is going to a whole new level, if you want it.

The restraining hand of the Holy Spirit is being lifted from both the places that do want Him, and the places that do not want Him. That is why schools are blowing up with violence, evil men are getting their way in war and crime, lust is being unrestrained in our media, and all sorts of darkness is increasing all around us. The harvest season is upon us. For those not denying themselves leadership of their own lives and going hard after the Spirit, the falling away must come:

2 Thessalonians 2:1-8 Now, brethren, concerning the coming of our Lord Jesus Christ and our gathering together to Him, we ask you, 2 not to be soon shaken in mind or troubled, either by spirit or by word or by letter, as if from us, as though the day of Christ had come. 3 Let no one deceive you by any means; for that Day will not come unless the falling away comes first, and the man of sin is revealed, the son of perdition, 4 who opposes and exalts himself above all that is called God or that is worshiped, so that he sits as God in the temple of God, showing himself that he is God. 5 Do you not remember that when I was still with you I told you these things? 6 And now you know what is restraining, that he may be revealed in his own time. 7 For the mystery of lawlessness is already at work; only He who now restrains will do so until He is taken out of the way. 8 And then the lawless one will be revealed, whom the Lord will consume with the breath of His mouth and destroy with the brightness of His coming.

This brings us to Sardis, the dead church. Jesus is giving the Sardis church a physical and finding that, though her great marketing is making the world think Sardis is alive, inside, she is dead. The Spirit has left the building. Let's look at the four-fold pattern for Sardis and see what Jesus is saying to the Church through His Spirit:

1. Jesus addresses Sardis as "He who has the seven Spirits of God and the seven stars."

Jesus comes to Sardis as the one who has the Holy Spirit, because that is what Sardis is lacking. She has uninvited the Spirit by not yielding to Him.

GOD WILL NOT COME TO OCCUPY SECOND PLACE. If you will not yield to Him in your mind, will, and emotions, He will not renew your mind, will, and emotions. Period.

Jesus HAS the Spirit. Jesus and the Spirit are ONE. Jesus is the one who has exactly what she needs. He also holds the "seven stars." The stars are the messengers to the churches. "Angels" in this passage can mean either supernatural or human messengers:

Revelation 1:20 This is the meaning of the mystery of the seven stars you saw in My right hand and the seven gold lampstands: The seven stars are the angels of the seven churches, and the seven lampstands are the seven churches.

Jesus is saying to Sardis that He is perfectly able to fill her with all the strength that comes with the leadership of the Spirit by giving the messengers to the church true information from heaven, true leadership right from the throne, if she wants it. BUT, in order to get it, she needs to decide where she wants a name, in heaven or in earth? Everyone gets what they want, and if Sardis wants her reputation to be in a dying earth, He will let her have it. But, if she finds her identity in a dying earth, she WILL die with it:

Matthew 16:24-27 Then Jesus said to His disciples, "If any of you wants to be My follower, you must turn from your selfish ways, take up your cross, and follow Me. 25 If you try to hang on to your life, you

will lose it. But if you give up your life for My sake, you will save it. 26 And what do you benefit if you gain the whole world but lose your own soul? Is anything worth more than your soul? 27 For the Son of Man will come with His angels in the glory of His Father and will judge all people according to their deeds.

Unlike the other churches in Revelation 2 and 3, each known for works, love, faith, and or service, Sardis is only commended for ONE thing. That brings us to the second part of the four-fold pattern:

2. "I know your works, that you have a name that you are alive, but you are dead.

Jesus says even her works, which are famous in the earth, are DEAD in His sight. Sardis only has her reputation among people, and a terrible reputation with Jesus. Isn't His opinion the point of doing church?

Programs designed in the heart of her man-pleasing leaders, all designed to make a name for herself, have given her a name in town, but inside she is dead. Though Sardis "sounds" power filled, the Spirit is NOT welcome to lead. Though a dying world thinks she is powerful, from the other side of the veil comes this truth "you are dead, and when the Bright Life of Mankind shows up, it will be plainly clear to everyone that you are dark and dead." Having a name among people is usually a sign that you DO NOT have a good reputation in heaven:

Luke 6:26 Woe to you when all men speak well of you, For so did their fathers to the false prophets.

Though everyone seems to think Sardis is the most amazing church in town, God has found her to be dead. But all is not lost. All she needs to do is repent that she might live before it is too late. That brings us to part 3 of the pattern, the correction:

3. *Be watchful, and strengthen the things which remain, that are
    ready to die, for I have not found your works perfect before God.
    3 Remember therefore how you have received and heard; hold
    fast and repent. Therefore if you will not watch, I will come upon
    you as a thief, and you will not know what hour I will come upon
    you. 4 You have a few names even in Sardis who have not
    defiled their garments; and they shall walk with Me in white, for
    they are worthy.*

God connects the death of Sardis --the casting off of the Spirit of God--
to Sardis' lack of "watching." Jesus is saying that Sardis is NOT paying
attention to the very specific thing He is doing, and this lack of vision
has caused her to "cast off restraint" that it requires, choice by choice,
to let the Spirit lead.

Remember, to be born again, we must deny the leadership of our mind,
will, and emotions and restrain our leadership to obedience to the
Spirit. This is true even when the Spirit is calling us to do, or say,
unpopular things. Without an understanding of what God is doing, this
process is tiresome. We fall asleep in the process. That is why Jesus
told the disciples to stay awake and pray. A time of trouble requires an
unusual response!!

**Mark 14:36-38 And He said, "Abba, Father, all things are possible for
You. Take this cup away from Me; nevertheless, not what I will, but
what You will." 37 Then He came and found them sleeping, and said
to Peter, "Simon, are you sleeping? Could you not <u>watch</u> one hour? 38
<u>Watch and pray</u>, lest you enter into temptation. The spirit indeed is
willing, but the flesh is weak."**

Jesus wanted Peter to understand the unique hour he was in. It
required "watching". That is why Revelation is so important. It gives us
the indicators in the Bible to connect to the news, called watching.
Without clear indications of progress, and a vision for where we are

going, we lose incentive to live restrained in the leadership of the Spirit and focused on the process God is working out in the time we most need it:

Proverbs 29:18 Where there is no revelation, the people cast off restraint; But happy is he who keeps the law.

Jesus didn't accidentally choose the name of the book of Revelation or the wording of this proverb. This is a direct warning about disregarding Revelation. Jesus stated it again in Revelation:

Revelation 1:3 Blessed is he who reads and those who hear the words of this prophecy, and keep those things which are written in it; for the time is near.

There is a reason that God appointed the Book of Revelation as the last book of the Bible. The Bible is the story of God restoring all that was lost in Genesis 3.   Genesis 1 and 2 is the story of what God desires in the earth: God with man, face to face, full of the Spirit, on a physical earth, with an open supernatural realm, heaven on earth. That is what God called very good, and God does not change. God is in the process of restoring "very good" for himself and anyone else who wants to call God with man "very good," too. God has chosen a BRILLIANT process to restore all that was lost and let the people of the earth choose for themselves whether they want in. Revelation is the MATURING of that process. That is where this whole thing is going.

Jesus says "WATCH" (Revelation 3:3) because you go where YOU are looking!

Sardis isn't reading the end time promises. They are doing their own thing, and Jesus says THAT is causing them to cast off the leadership of the Holy Spirit and try to squeeze every last drop from their man-based logic and marketing plan.   Their focus on the world has caused them to miss the plain and obvious fact that they are dying in a time when everyone should be growing in life by growing in the leadership of the Spirit.

Sardis uses the warning of Jesus "no one knows the day or hour" as an excuse to NOT watch. This is actually blasphemy! This statement has become one of the most common expressions of the lack of being led by the Spirit and instead leading from your own logic. Using this phrase..."no one knows the day or hour"...to do nothing is actually speaking judgment over yourself. If you are the leader of a church, using this expression to take comfort to NOT watch is speaking judgment over your whole church. You must repent if you have used Jesus' warning as an excuse to do nothing:

Revelation 3:3 Remember therefore how you have received and heard; hold fast and repent. Therefore if you will not watch, I will come upon you as a thief, and you will not know what hour I will come upon you.

Jesus' coming will seem like you have been stolen from if you will not watch. That means refusing to watch will result in much loss for you, your family, and your church. To watch you must know the Word and declare what you see as the Word connects with the news of the day.

You must stand for the truth as revealed by the Spirit through the Word. Remember Pergamos? They had the Spirit without the Word. They were about to blow up. Sardis has the exact opposite problem. They lack the Spirit and are not even praised for the Word. They are drying up and don't even have the Word anymore. All they have is a reputation that is no longer accurate, if it ever was. It takes the Spirit and the Word to grow up...to live again.

The Spirit does things that offend the mind. The Word says things that are unpopular. The Spirit is not good for popularity contests. But, the

Spirit is the one who searches the deep things of God. The Holy Spirit gives us counsel to the right and to the left, when no one else knows what to do. Confusion is guaranteed to increase. This will create great intensity. There are two kinds of people who will be present on the earth at the time the trouble breaks out: those caught up in the world and those who are seeking God with their whole heart as their ONE THING. The presence of God is the safe place to be in the time of trouble:

Psalms 27:4-6 One thing I have desired of the LORD, That will I seek: That I may dwell in the house of the LORD All the days of my life, To behold the beauty of the LORD, And to inquire in His temple. 5 For in the time of trouble He shall hide me in His pavilion; In the secret place of His tabernacle He shall hide me; He shall set me high upon a rock. 6 And now my head shall be lifted up above my enemies all around me; Therefore I will offer sacrifices of joy in His tabernacle; I will sing, yes, I will sing praises to the LORD.

The generation that agrees with this formula for safety is called the "generation of Jacob" in the Bible. They are the ones who want to see God's face, and they will literally open the heavens with their desire to see God. An "opening of heaven" is great for those that are ready, and terrible for those that are not. You get ready by making your life entirely about seeing God. This causes you, in earnest zeal and desire, to hunger and thirst for clean hands and a pure heart. This causes you to choose holiness because you are literally watching for heaven to start opening as you press in. Jesus is returning to people that respond to Him. That is what it means for the King of Glory to come in:

Psalms 24:1-10 A Psalm of David. The earth is the LORD's, and all its fullness, The world and those who dwell therein. 2 For He has founded it upon the seas, And established it upon the waters. 3 Who may ascend into the hill of the LORD? Or who may stand in His holy place? 4 He who has clean hands and a pure heart, Who has not lifted

up his soul to an idol, Nor sworn deceitfully. 5 He shall receive
blessing from the LORD, And righteousness from the God of his
salvation. 6 This is Jacob, the generation of those who seek Him, Who
seek Your face. Selah 7 Lift up your heads, O you gates! And be lifted
up, you everlasting doors! And the King of glory shall come in. 8 Who
is this King of glory? The LORD strong and mighty, The LORD mighty in
battle. 9 Lift up your heads, O you gates! Lift up, you everlasting
doors! And the King of glory shall come in. 10 Who is this King of
glory? The LORD of hosts, He is the King of glory. Selah

This is describing a ready, watching, and actively responding people.
But, if you are not ready, if you are not actively growing in holiness by
drawing the Spirit into your mind, will, and emotions both individually
and as a church you will be afraid as heaven opens. If you are
lackadaisical in searching what the Spirit is saying to you in this hour
because you have not studied Jesus' end time plan, you will be terrified
as heaven opens. If you aren't seeking His face with cleaner hands and
ever purer hearts, you will, in SHAME, hide from His face:

Revelation 6:12-17 I looked when He opened the sixth seal, and
behold, there was a great earthquake; and the sun became black as
sackcloth of hair, and the moon became like blood. 13 And the stars
of heaven fell to the earth, as a fig tree drops its late figs when it is
shaken by a mighty wind. 14 Then the sky receded as a scroll when it
is rolled up, and every mountain and island was moved out of its place.
15 And the kings of the earth, the great men, the rich men, the
commanders, the mighty men, every slave and every free man, hid
themselves in the caves and in the rocks of the mountains, 16 and
said to the mountains and rocks, "Fall on us and hide us from the face
of Him who sits on the throne and from the wrath of the Lamb! 17 For
the great day of His wrath has come, and who is able to stand?"

Who is able to stand? That should be the question of our hour. Jesus
says "listen to what the Spirit says to the churches if you want to stand."

If you want to hide and be terrified in the next years coming, go ahead and keep listening to your own heart and grading yourself by how many people agree with you, come to your meetings, or talk about you as "anointed." If you aren't seeking God and keeping yourself for His evaluation of you, you will hide with those same people behind rocks when God's glory appears. Everyone gets what they want.

In His mercy, Jesus has planted, as missionaries, those who have are Spirit-led, contending for holiness by the Spirit, in the churches with great reputations but no life:

Revelation 3:4 You have a few names even in Sardis who have not defiled their garments; and they shall walk with Me in white, for they are worthy.

These are the ones who keep throwing the wrenches in the cogs of your man-pleasing programs. They say "shouldn't we pray?" or "what is the Spirit saying?" These are the ones who don't care about what logic says. They say "if God brought us to this, He will take us through this." These faithful ones say "I hear the Lord saying we should go this unpopular way" They are led by the Spirit, which is much different than being led by man-based wisdom and a man-pleasing spirit. These faithful ones are much more concerned about offending God and missing what He is doing, than they are about offending people, especially pastors. These gems are like gold dust sprinkled among you. If you will listen to them, they will help your whole church revive. They are the mercy of God sent to you. But, if you disregard them, you will die while they still live. If you want to live where they live, you must live like they live.

That brings us to the reward for overcoming. This is the promise available to the Spiritless church if she will repent and stand for truth:

4. *He who overcomes shall be clothed in white garments, and I will not blot out his name from the Book of Life; but I will confess his name before My Father and before His angels.*

The process of Jesus returning is a process. Impatience will not endure this hour. You cannot gauge your success by what people think or say about you.   If God is your source AND your reward, you will stand.

Jesus, by the information in Revelation, has promised to remove every man-based strength from the earth in order to judge the inadequacy of anything less than relying on God's manna-producing, water-from-the-rock, moment by moment leadership. You need to be as rooted in Him and His leadership as possible. To be saved, yet remain rooted in the world's ways, is a recipe to fall away, to wither, and to die:

Luke 8:13 But the ones on the rock are those who, when they hear, receive the word with joy; and these have no root, who believe for a while and in time of temptation fall away.

He who has an ear, let him hear what the Spirit says to the churches.

Chapter 7 – Philadelphia

"The Church That Opens Heaven"

Revelation 3:7-13 "And to the angel of the church in Philadelphia write, 'These things says He who is holy, He who is true, "HE WHO HAS THE KEY OF DAVID, HE WHO OPENS AND NO ONE SHUTS, AND SHUTS AND NO ONE OPENS": 8 "I know your works. See, I have set before you an open door, and no one can shut it; for you have a little strength, have kept My word, and have not denied My name. 9 Indeed I will make those of the synagogue of Satan, who say they are Jews and are not, but lie—indeed I will make them come and worship before your feet, and to know that I have loved you. 10 Because you have kept My command to persevere, I also will keep you from the hour of trial which shall come upon the whole world, to test those who dwell on the earth. 11 Behold, I am coming quickly! Hold fast what you have, that no one may take your crown. 12 He who overcomes, I will make him a pillar in the temple of My God, and he shall go out no more. I will write on him the name of My God and the name of the city of My God, the New Jerusalem, which comes down out of heaven from My God. And I will write on him My new name. 13 "He who has an ear, let him hear what the Spirit says to the churches."

Philadelphia, the church of "brotherly love," is all about "David's key." Philadelphia is the only one of all the seven churches that was not currently in tribulation and also not corrected by Jesus. This is because they were full of the very thing Jesus addressed them with. Let's jump into the four-fold pattern for Philadelphia and see what Jesus wants US to know in this hour:

1. Jesus addresses Philadelphia as He who is holy, He who is true,
    "HE WHO HAS THE KEY OF DAVID, HE WHO OPENS AND NO ONE
    SHUTS, AND SHUTS AND NO ONE OPENS

Holiness and truth are the foundation of the Philadelphia church, and
on that desire for holiness and truth sprang up the same thing that
came out of David's one desire for holiness and truth. This is David's
Key. You MUST understand what David's Key is if you want to agree
with Jesus about His end time plan.

Let me say it clearly: David's key is night and day prayer to music, called
the Tabernacle of David in the Bible.

David hired 24,000 people to keep night and day worship and prayer
going in Jerusalem. This was the foundation of David's government.
This was the foundation of David's "throne." Jesus is going to govern the
earth in the same way, sitting on the same throne, or governmental
seat, as His ancestor David. That is what the angel Gabriel told Mary
before Jesus was born:

*Luke 1:30-32 Then the angel said to her, "Do not be afraid, Mary, for
you have found favor with God. 31 And behold, you will conceive in
your womb and bring forth a Son, and shall call His name JESUS. 32 He
will be great, and will be called the Son of the Highest; and the Lord
God will give Him the throne of His father David*.

Night and Day prayer was David's "key" because it unlocked heaven
over Israel. David sought God's kingdom first, as a governmental
strategy, and God gave David all the rest, in addition to showing David
how to worship on earth as God is worshiped in heaven:

Matthew 6:31-33 "Therefore do not worry, saying, 'What shall we eat?' or 'What shall we drink?' or 'What shall we wear?' 32 For after all these things the Gentiles seek. For your heavenly Father knows that you need all these things. 33 But seek first the kingdom of God and His righteousness, and all these things shall be added to you.

David understood this truth spoken by Jesus and practically expressed it in Jerusalem by organizing a ton of people to keep prayer going night and day in the geography assigned to him. Using David's Key was a COLLECTIVE effort, and it turned Jerusalem into God's Holy Mountain. Specifically, it turned Arauhna's threshing floor, a place where David wrestled with God and had his heart sifted, into the Temple Mount (you can read about that in 2 Samuel 24 and 2 Chronicles 3:1). The Temple was simply a permanent location for what David had started in a tent: a system of night and day prayer that was the basis of David's government. Even David's military guys had a part in the organization of the tabernacle, where worship leaders would take turns leading night and day worship in Israel:

1 Chronicles 25:1-8 Moreover David and the <u>captains of the army</u> separated for the service some of the sons of Asaph, of Heman, and of Jeduthun, who should prophesy with harps, stringed instruments, and cymbals. And the number of the skilled men performing their service was: 2 Of the sons of Asaph: Zaccur, Joseph, Nethaniah, and Asharelah; the sons of Asaph were under the direction of Asaph, who prophesied according to the order of the king. 3 Of Jeduthun, the sons of Jeduthun: Gedaliah, Zeri, Jeshaiah, Shimei, Hashabiah, and Mattithiah, six, under the direction of their father Jeduthun, who prophesied with a harp to give thanks and to praise the LORD. 4 Of Heman, the sons of Heman: Bukkiah, Mattaniah, Uzziel, Shebuel, Jerimoth, Hananiah, Hanani, Eliathah, Giddalti, Romamti-Ezer, Joshbekashah, Mallothi, Hothir, and Mahazioth. 5 All these were the sons of Heman the king's seer in the words of God, to exalt his horn. For God gave Heman fourteen sons and three daughters. 6 All these were under the direction of their father for the music in the house of

the LORD, with cymbals, stringed instruments, and harps, for the
service of the house of God. Asaph, Jeduthun, and Heman were under
the authority of the king. 7 So the number of them, with their brethren
who were instructed in the songs of the LORD, all who were skillful,
was two hundred and eighty-eight. 8 And they cast lots for their duty,
the small as well as the great, the teacher with the student.

David's tabernacle was highly organized and included participation from
the entire community. This opened heaven over Israel in a very
profound way. Those worship leaders listed in 1 Chronicles 25 are some
famous people in the Bible. They are the authors of many of the
Psalms. The Psalms contain the largest prophetic release earth had seen
to that date. Before the Spirit was poured out on the believers in the
upper room in Jerusalem in Acts 2, David's night and day worship teams
were regularly singing prophetically. 4,000 prophetic singers and
musicians pressed the veil between heaven and earth day and night,
and did not come away empty-handed!

David took the key of night and day worship, and opened a door
between heaven and earth that released the greatest prophetic insight
the earth had seen up to that time. Using David's Key also created an
abundance of peace, and stability, and an outpouring of resources that
left Solomon, the one who put the tabernacle in the Temple, the
wealthiest and wisest king earth has ever seen. This is what night and
day prayer, as expressed by God's people in a community, is all about.
This is David's Key. Jesus celebrates the fact that Philadelphia has
chosen what looks like weakness to be their strength. Jesus' unusual
plan is actually brilliantly strong:

2.   *Revelation 3:8 "I know your works. See, I have set before you an*
     open door, and no one can shut it; for you have a little strength,
     have kept My word, and have not denied My name. 9 Indeed I
     will make those of the synagogue of Satan, who say they are
     Jews and are not, but lie—indeed I will make them come and

worship before your feet, and to know that I have loved you.

Worship is the weapon required in the end times. Specifically, night and day worship is what the Bible describes as the end time plan for Jesus' Bride. This offends many who say they know God. Jesus said that those who are unwilling to humble themselves and bless David's Key will worship one way or the other.

When I first heard about night and day prayer, I thought it was very unusual, maybe even cultish. It seemed like a weird way for people to spend their time. I had been in the church for nearly 40 years and had never heard ONE teaching about night and day prayer. What I have come to realize is that, although night and day prayer to music was a very established reality for the early Church, it has been lost along the way. This was actually prophesied in Revelation 2 and 3! That is why, according to Jesus, five of the seven churches are veering far from the narrow road of obedience.

The church in these last days is in bad shape, according to the Bible. As I have said before, according to the Bible, seventy one percent of the Church, or five of the seven churches in Revelation 2 and 3, are so out of whack that if they don't repent and come into agreement with Jesus about what is required to endure the Tribulation, they will fall away. Of those, two churches not corrected by God, and one of them (Smyrna) is currently already IN tribulation! That leaves only one church standing as a shining example of how to "get safe in a time of trouble." That is why I am writing this book!

Trouble is coming, friends, and if you want to know the ONLY BIBLICAL WAY to prepare yourself, your family, your church, and your city to be safe in the storm coming, you must humble yourself and consider what the Spirit is saying about Philadelphia.

The more I have studied night and day prayer in the Bible, the more it has become painfully and gloriously clear to me that this concept is one of the most established concepts in the Bible, but to a modern western-mindset Christian, it is unusual. I did not like it at first. I did not want to believe it at first. I didn't like the end time eschatology connected to it at first. But, after I humbled myself and began saying to Jesus "if this is your plan, show me," what I found is that this is, in fact, Jesus end time plan for His Church. A night and day praying city led into this reality by a faithful Bride coming together in unity is the ONLY safe place in the storm that is coming. The benefits for agreeing with God about this are so overwhelming it is hard to cover them in one book, let alone one chapter. This bears intensive study. Once you see it, you cannot un-see it! Understanding this simple truth will unlock huge portions of the scripture in new ways. It will excite your heart, if you let it.

Jesus' unusual plans are wise, and they always succeed. Jesus has not brought us to this time and this place to fail, but to win! But, everyone has to choose for themselves if they will humble themselves and agree with God about what strategy actually wins! Humility is required because Jesus' plan is very unusual by design! We live in a very unique hour. This is the proper time for the harvest, it is the time for the "unusual act" of the Lord to be performed through His people that He prophesied through Isaiah:

Isaiah 28:21-29 For the LORD will rise up as at Mount Perazim, He will be angry as in the Valley of Gibeon— That He may do His work, His awesome work, And bring to pass His act, His <u>*unusual act*</u>*. 22 Now therefore, do not be mockers, Lest your bonds be made strong; For I have heard from the Lord GOD of hosts, A destruction determined even upon the whole earth. 23 Give ear and hear my voice, Listen and hear my speech. 24 Does the plowman keep plowing all day to sow? Does he keep turning his soil and breaking the clods? 25 When he has leveled its surface, Does he not sow the black cummin And scatter the cummin, Plant the wheat in rows, The barley in the appointed place, And the spelt in its place? 26 For He instructs him in right judgment,*

His God teaches him. 27 For the black cummin is not threshed with a threshing sledge, Nor is a cartwheel rolled over the cummin; But the black cummin is beaten out with a stick, And the cummin with a rod. 28 Bread flour must be ground; Therefore he does not thresh it forever, Break it with his cartwheel, Or crush it with his horsemen. 29 This also comes from the LORD of hosts, Who is wonderful in counsel and excellent in guidance.

The plans and the timing of the Lord are very important. This is why watching is so important. Entertainment, and the cares of this dying world, have stolen the attention of many of God's people. It is time to turn off the distractions and get busy studying God's end time plans. Your life literally depends on it. It is a judgment on the church in America that I am one of the very rare voices telling you this, but that doesn't make it any less true. Don't take my word for it, though. That would be a big mistake. Search the Word yourself. Ask Jesus to show you if this is true. Searching the Word is what will fill your heart with zeal.

If you aren't fully invested in what Jesus is doing, you WILL miss it. That is what we talked about for Sardis. Jesus' plan is unusual and requires an active searching of the Word with the Spirit and connecting it to the events around you. This is called "watching":

Luke 21:34-36 "But take heed to yourselves, lest your hearts be weighed down with carousing, drunkenness, and cares of this life, and that Day come on you unexpectedly. 35 For it will come as a snare on all those who dwell on the face of the whole earth. 36 Watch therefore, and pray always that you may be counted worthy to escape all these things that will come to pass, and to stand before the Son of Man."

"Praying always," like in David's Israel, is the answer. But, the "cares of this life" are the main focus of most of the church in America.

Congregations led by false teachers, the synagogue of satan that Jesus spoke to Philadelphia about, want you to believe that following Jesus is mostly about improving your experience in the "cares of this life" --doing stuff, or doing nothing-- anything but giving yourself wholeheartedly to worship. Woe to those false shepherds and those that follow them. They will worship at Philadelphia's feet, because Philadelphia is the one church who actually searched Jesus' heart, and, in humility, accepted what they found.

Jesus is actually crying out "cast off the cares of this so-called life if you actually want to live!" This requires turning off the distractions and getting fascinated with the man who has longed for thousands of years for the hour we get to live in. Wake up sleepers!

This requirement to choose wholeheartedly to understand Jesus' plan is actually an important component of Jesus' plan. The humility required is part of the way He sifts the true Bride out of the earth. Jesus is singing a song, and only those that love Him will break from what they are doing, follow the music and come sing with Him. Many who claim to love Him are not even listening for His melody. Instead of searching His heart, like a loving spouse, many are most interested in how Jesus is going to benefit them now, like a harlot. The prostitute does what the wife is supposed to do, but does it for pay. This calls for repentance. A washing off of the stain of self and getting purer hands and a cleaner heart is required. Anyone can begin entering in to purity...getting washed and ready for the wedding, but you must choose it for yourself. The Bride gets Herself ready. This is for love. Jesus will not force anyone to their own wedding:

Revelation 19:7-8 Let us be glad and rejoice and give Him glory, for the marriage of the Lamb has come, and His wife has made herself ready." 8 And to her It was granted to be arrayed in fine linen, clean and bright, for the fine linen is the righteous acts of the saints.

The Bride must choose to make herself ready. But, this isn't the full story. We don't get ready alone. Jesus, the wealthy groom, has all of the power to help His Bride become ready. He is the owner of the land, which means He organizes the circumstances of the earth to give His Bride the "perfect chamber" to prepare. Jesus will not violate His Bride's free will, He will not violate love, but He commands the wind and the waves to do just what is necessary to give her great incentive to move her through the process. The Bride makes herself ready, but Jesus gives her the "brush and curling iron", and the perfect room to be ready:

Ephesians 5:25-27 Husbands, love your wives, just as Christ also loved the church and gave Himself for her, 26 that He might sanctify and cleanse her with the washing of water by the word, 27 that He might present her to Himself a glorious church, not having spot or wrinkle or any such thing, but that she should be holy and without blemish.

Right now, the intensity of the world is heating up. This is no accident! This is the zeal of the Groom in action. This is the sifting process God has selected in order to sift out a Bride, the true harvest, for His Son. God is the one orchestrating the events of the earth. He will never let go. In fact, He will grip it harder and shake everything that can be shaken. The shaking IS the threshing process. This is the time of testing Jesus warns all of the churches of, but God tells Philadelphia her choices to agree with Him about real strength are what will keep her through this time:

3. *Revelation 3:10 Because you have kept My command to persevere, I also will keep you from the hour of trial which shall come upon the whole world, to test those who dwell on the earth. 11 Behold, I am coming quickly! Hold fast what you have, that no one may take your crown.*

God is throwing all things into the wind of the end time events to test them to see what blows away. This is the harvest process that separates the wheat from the chaff, called "threshing." This process is just beginning, it will get much more intense. But, make no mistake, the enemy armies of the earth are not getting away with anything. They are being used by Jesus, just as Nebuchadnezzar was used by the Lord to sift Israel. Jesus isn't forcing the revived Islamic Caliphate to rise up and dominate the earth, He is removing His hand of restraint to allow lawless men and women to get what they want. Jesus never lets go of the earth. The Lord is at the head of the column of the enemy armies. This should comfort those truly loyal to Jesus. Joel prophesied this very truth:

Joel 2:1-11 Blow the trumpet in Zion, And sound an alarm in My holy mountain! Let all the inhabitants of the land tremble; For the day of the LORD is coming, For it is at hand: 2 A day of darkness and gloominess, A day of clouds and thick darkness, Like the morning clouds spread over the mountains. A people come, great and strong, The like of whom has never been; Nor will there ever be any such after them, Even for many successive generations. 3 A fire devours before them, And behind them a flame burns; The land is like the Garden of Eden before them, And behind them a desolate wilderness; Surely nothing shall escape them. 4 Their appearance is like the appearance of horses; And like swift steeds, so they run. 5 With a noise like chariots Over mountaintops they leap, Like the noise of a flaming fire that devours the stubble, Like a strong people set in battle array. 6 Before them the people writhe in pain; All faces are drained of color. 7 They run like mighty men, They climb the wall like men of war; Every one marches in formation, And they do not break ranks. 8 They do not push one another; Every one marches in his own column. Though they lunge between the weapons, They are not cut down. 9 They run to and fro in the city, They run on the wall; They climb into the houses, They enter at the windows like a thief. 10 The earth quakes before them, The heavens tremble; The sun and moon grow dark, And the stars diminish their brightness. 11 The LORD gives voice before His army, For His camp is very great; For strong is the One who executes His word.

For the day of the LORD is great and very terrible; <u>Who can endure it?</u>

Who can stand? Who can endure? This is the question before all the earth. This is the test, and the answer is clear in numerous places in the Bible. The answer is night and day prayer, or the tabernacle of David. This is actually the only clear and consistent answer to the trouble.

Those who can stand are the "generation of Jacob," those who respond in humility and do the "unusual thing" that Jesus requires. That is what Jacob did. Jacob wrestled with God at Peniel. Wrestled with God??!! Yes, and He received the blessing in the very place heaven opens:

Genesis 32:24-30 Then Jacob was left alone; and a Man wrestled with him until the breaking of day. 25 Now when He saw that He did not prevail against him, He touched the socket of his hip; and the socket of Jacob's hip was out of joint as He wrestled with him. 26 And He said, "Let Me go, for the day breaks." But he said, "I will not let You go unless You bless me!" 27 So He said to him, "What is your name?" He said, "Jacob." 28 And He said, "Your name shall no longer be called Jacob, but Israel; for you have <u>struggled with God and with men</u>, and have prevailed." 29 Then Jacob asked, saying, "Tell me Your name, I pray." And He said, "Why is it that you ask about My name?" And He blessed him there. 30 So Jacob called the name of the place Peniel: "<u>For I have seen God face to face, and my life is preserved</u>."

Jacob was not the best dude. If you know His story, you know His story is one of redemption, and it is all related to how he became Israel, God's man. Jacob was named Israel by the wrestling. By the responding. He wrestled not just with God, but with God and men. That is what Jesus is orchestrating for an entire generation in our hour. Do you see it? Do you see how suddenly evil men are getting more successful at their evil plans and desires? This is intentional. We live in the harvest hour.

God is allowing the wheat and tares to fully mature. This is great for the righteous and terrible for the evil. In our hour the earth is being ushered into a divine setup to see who is willing to wrestle for the blessing, knowing by faith that God is good and will reward the righteous. It is a harvest of faith. Faith requires a response:

Hebrews 11:7 By faith Noah, being divinely warned of things not yet seen, moved with godly fear, prepared an ark for the saving of his household, by which he condemned the world and became heir of the righteousness which is according to faith.

Everyone will get what they want. Those who want God and to ascend His "Holy Mountain" will get success in reaching the pinnacle. The pinnacle of the mountain of God is the opening of heaven...doing the same works as Jesus, and even greater works, is the initial measure of heaven opening. The fullness of heaven opening at the end of this age is Jesus returning, but Jesus is only coming back to a Bride who has prepared herself in love as demonstrated by her obedience. We call that holiness:

John 14:12-15 "Most assuredly, I say to you, he who believes in Me, the works that I do he will do also; and greater works than these he will do, because I go to My Father. 13 And whatever you ask in My name, that I will do, that the Father may be glorified in the Son. 14 If you ask anything in My name, I will do it. 15 "If you love Me, keep My commandments.

This is the most glorious news for our generation, because the trouble, the sifting we are beginning to see, is evidence that if we will respond, we are the generation that will literally open heaven and see Jesus face to face. According to the Bible, the Bride that is like Philadelphia will prepare a throne for the King of Kings on her night and day praise, and that very act will open heaven for her groom to come. A door no one can shut. God is enthroned on the praises of HIS people. David prophesied that His Son, the Messiah, would go to the cross with this on His mind:

Psalms 22:1-5 To the Chief Musician. Set to "The Deer of the Dawn." a Psalm of David. My God, My God, why have You forsaken Me? Why are You so far from helping Me, And from the words of My groaning? 2 O My God, <u>I cry in the daytime</u>, but You do not hear; <u>And in the night</u> season, and am not silent. 3 <u>But You are holy, Enthroned in the praises of Israel.</u> 4 Our fathers trusted in You; They trusted, and You delivered them. 5 They cried to You, and were delivered; They trusted in You, and were not ashamed.

When Jesus went to the cross, when He cried out "Father, why have you forsaken me," what was driving Him? It was this vision of the people of the earth once again preparing a throne for the father in night and day prayer to music, called praise. Revelation ends with the Father's throne back in the garden He called "very good" in Genesis 1. Jesus describes His wrestling, His own praying in the day and praying in the night, even though it looked like nothing was happening. Jesus saw clearly why the night and day cry matters. Faith let Him gaze on the truth that God is actually being enthroned on His very wrestling!

The past history of God's people trusting God and experiencing deliverance in the small measure has built confidence that God will not let His holy one taste shame. This is why Jesus obeyed the Father, even to His own humiliation and death, look what it says later in Psalm 22:

Psalms 22:23 You who fear the LORD, praise Him! <u>All you descendants of Jacob, glorify Him</u>, And fear Him, all you offspring of Israel!

We live in the hour of the generation that responds, the generation where the descendants of God, the sons of God, the offspring of Jacob, will obey this command from Messiah, will rise up, throw off the comforts of the earth, and open heaven in the costly act of night and day prayer:

Romans 8:18-19 For I consider that the sufferings of this present time are not worthy to be compared with the glory which shall be revealed in us. 19 For the earnest expectation of the <u>creation eagerly waits for the revealing of the sons of God</u>.

This is the pinnacle, or the end of the narrow road Jesus, the firstborn of many, walked for us. Jesus is the WAY. We are supposed to follow Him right to the cross of Psalm 22:1-5.

This is ALL about night and day prayer in the communities of the earth, called in the Bible, the "mountains," being the places where the true sons of God prove themselves by their response to the testing of the Tribulation. The Psalm 24 mountains or hills of God are the locations of the earth where the people build the night and day praying churches...the Philadelphia churches...that will provide refuge to the end time family of God through the Great Tribulation. This act of obedience to the unusual plan of God is what will "keep" the Bride through the storm. Psalm 72 prophesies this very truth for our generation:

Psalms 72:1-3 A Psalm Of Solomon. Give the king Your judgments, O God, And Your righteousness to the king's Son. 2 He will judge Your people with righteousness, And Your poor with justice. 3 <u>The mountains will bring peace to the people, And the little hills, by righteousness.</u>

This is an end-time passage about the judgments of God being released. God's judgments are REALLY good for people that are right with God, because they stop unjust evil against them!! But ask yourself, how do mountains bring peace?! Solomon was singing about the same mountains his dad, David, had prophesied for the sons of God to arise to:

Psalms 24:1-10 A Psalm of David. The earth is the LORD's, and all its fullness, The world and those who dwell therein. 2 For He has founded it upon the seas, And established it upon the waters. 3 <u>Who may ascend into the hill of the LORD?</u> Or who may stand in His holy place? 4 He who has clean hands and a pure heart, Who has not lifted up his soul to an idol, Nor sworn deceitfully. 5 He shall receive blessing from the LORD, And righteousness from the God of his salvation. 6 <u>This is Jacob, the generation of those who seek Him, Who seek Your face.</u> Selah 7 Lift up your heads, O you gates! And <u>be lifted up, you everlasting doors! And the King of glory shall come in</u>. 8 Who is this King of glory? The LORD strong and mighty, The LORD mighty in battle. 9 Lift up your heads, O you gates! Lift up, you everlasting doors! And the King of glory shall come in. 10 Who is this King of glory? The LORD of hosts, He is the King of glory. Selah

The generation of Jacob will ascend "holy mountains" all over the earth by "seeking God's face" as their main occupation, for real. This will create hilltop cities of safety, or cities of refuge, all over the earth. This has already begun. Many are learning to do this day by day, as thousands of night and day worship centers are rising up all over the earth. These faithful sons and daughters of God will still work, they aren't hunkering down in bunkers with guns and food. They are out in the open, living through the realities of life, but they will take shifts keeping a night and day cry to God going until heaven opens and Jesus comes down like He went up! This is becoming their one desire, and as that happens, as they seek God as their one thing, they are creating a safe place in the time of trouble. This is what David's Key is primarily about:

Psalms 27:4-5 One thing I have desired of the LORD, That will I seek: That I may dwell in the house of the LORD All the days of my life, To behold the beauty of the LORD, And to inquire in His temple. 5 For in the time of trouble He shall hide me in His pavilion; In the secret place of His tabernacle He shall hide me; He shall set me high upon a rock.

What this night and day cry, called in Joel 2 a "solemn assembly," will do is heal the land in the mountains themselves and open heaven over these locations. The opening of heaven will actually be like a "force field" that keeps the antichrist armies away and begins the process of the glory of God actually breaking through to earth. The glory of God is the light of His countenance. Jesus, in all His glory, is very bright. So bright that if the earth saw Him in His glory, it would consume everything not ready to encounter Him:

1 Timothy 6:12-16 Fight the good fight of faith, lay hold on eternal life, to which you were also called and have confessed the good confession in the presence of many witnesses. 13 I urge you in the sight of God who gives life to all things, and before Christ Jesus who witnessed the good confession before Pontius Pilate, 14 that you keep this commandment without spot, blameless until our Lord Jesus Christ's appearing, 15 which He will manifest in His own time, He who is the blessed and only Potentate, the King of kings and Lord of lords, 16 who alone has immortality, dwelling in unapproachable light, whom no man has seen or can see, to whom be honor and everlasting power. Amen.

This light coming into the darkness is very terrible for darkness. That is the other side of the story. Everyone is going to get what they want. If you want God to be your everything, you are in for a really good time, because this activity of making God your one thing, growing in purity, will actually work:

Matthew 5:8 Blessed are the pure in heart, For they shall see God.

Those climbing the holy mountains, getting a vision for how night and day prayer will open heaven over a community, then putting on a hunger and thirst for holiness as their ONE desire, and letting the rest of life trail behind that seeking the kingdom first, will literally begin opening heaven and encountering God in the physical realm. This has happened in small ways all over the earth for centuries. In the last 200 years, places like Herrnhut, Germany; Moravian Falls, NC; Almolonga, Guatemala, and many others, have tasted the initial release of heaven opening in response to night and day prayer. When night and day prayer happens in agreement with God, angelic encounters increase, the land produces more food, and peace rests on the land where there was violence. Look further into Psalm 72, and you will see this same promise for the mountains:

Psalms 72:16 There will be an abundance of grain in the earth, <u>On the top of the mountains</u>; Its fruit shall wave like Lebanon; And <u>those of the city shall flourish</u> like grass of the earth.

I don't know if you know anything about geography, but crops don't grow on the tops of natural mountains! Natural mountains are pointy, rocky, and sometimes covered in snow. This prophetic Psalm is talking about the mountains of God that David prophesied for the generation of Jacob. These are the geographic locations that build the end time Tabernacles of David, as a community. This is God's unusual plan: to orchestrate trouble in the earth so that those who love Him will agree that trouble must come to judge sin, and they will respond by rebuilding David's Tabernacle, the safe mountains of God, all over the earth:

Amos 9:8-15 "Behold, the eyes of the Lord GOD are on the sinful kingdom, And I will destroy it from the face of the earth; Yet I <u>will not utterly destroy the house of Jacob</u>," Says the LORD. 9 "For surely I will command, And will <u>sift the house of Israel among all nations</u>, As grain is sifted in a sieve; <u>Yet not the smallest grain shall fall to the ground</u>. 10 All the sinners of My people shall die by the sword, Who say, 'The calamity shall not overtake nor confront us.' 11 "On that day <u>I will raise up The tabernacle of David</u>, which has fallen down, And repair its damages; I will raise up its ruins, And rebuild it as in the days of old; 12

That they may possess the remnant of Edom, And all the Gentiles who are called by My name," Says the LORD who does this thing. 13 "Behold, the days are coming," says the LORD, "When the plowman shall overtake the reaper, And the treader of grapes him who sows seed; The mountains shall drip with sweet wine, And all the hills shall flow with it. 14 I will bring back the captives of My people Israel; They shall build the waste cities and inhabit them; They shall plant vineyards and drink wine from them; They shall also make gardens and eat fruit from them. 15 I will plant them in their land, And no longer shall they be pulled up From the land I have given them," Says the LORD your God.

You really want to be safe in what is coming like a flood to earth. What we are seeing in the Middle East right now is prophesied to spread. A man is promising to be the answer to the trouble, and out of impatient desperation, the people of the earth will empower him. God will give the earth what she wants, and this man will show himself for who he is, which is the end time culmination of the evil men the earth has already put her trust in. To choose the strength of a man over wholehearted seeking of God is rebellion.

Those who want rebellion will get success for an hour. The success of rebellion, which is living outside of a relationship with the true leader of all creation, is death. And death is coming friends. Unfortunately for the people of the earth, much death is coming. Stage one is the death of over a quarter of the earth's population, that is nearly 2 billion people, in less than approximately 3 years:

Revelation 6:8 So I looked, and behold, a pale horse. And the name of him who sat on it was Death, and Hades followed with him. And power was given to them over a fourth of the earth, to kill with sword, with hunger, with death, and by the beasts of the earth.

Stage two is the death of another one third of the earth's population in approximately 5 months:

Revelation 9:18 By these three plagues a third of mankind was killed— by the fire and the smoke and the brimstone which came out of their mouths.

That means in less than 1,260 days, one half of the earth's population will be killed by God giving to mankind what they desire: the leadership of a man, called the antichrist, to give the peace, prosperity, and security, and then, when the earth will not repent, giving them the leadership of satan and his demons for approximately 5 months (Revelation 9:5).

Rather than participate in what invisible God is doing, at least half of the earth wants a tangible politician to give them what they want. Behind that politician is satan. In the seal judgments, God will allow the antichrist, the man the earth loves, to have his way. What the earth will get when antichrist gets his way is the same thing she has always gotten when she has looked for a man to divide up the resources of the earth for her: war, famine, pestilence, and widespread death, with only a few at the top holding all the resources. We know these famous men that have promised hope and change to the earth: Hitler, Lenin, Stalin, Mao, Castro, Chavez. These ones were allowed limited success as a warning to the earth. The antichrist will be given authority over much more of the earth than those previous men for 42 months (1,260 days):

Revelation 13:4-8 So they worshiped the dragon who gave authority to the beast; and they worshiped the beast, saying, "Who is like the beast? Who is able to make war with him?" 5 And he was given a mouth speaking great things and blasphemies, and <u>he was given authority to continue for forty-two months.</u> 6 Then he opened his mouth in blasphemy against God, to blaspheme His name, His tabernacle, and those who dwell in heaven. 7 It was granted to him to

make war with the saints and to overcome them. And authority was given him over every tribe, tongue, and nation. 8 All who dwell on the earth will worship him, whose names have not been written in the Book of Life of the Lamb slain from the foundation of the world.

This is part of the testing that will require <u>vengeance</u> (remember this word, I'll come back to it in a minute) be brought when Jesus returns. Jesus is going to return and take vengeance on the antichrist. How? By shining the bright light of His glory and singing His song of victory:

2 Thessalonians 2:1-8 Now, brethren, concerning the coming of our Lord Jesus Christ and our gathering together to Him, we ask you, 2 not to be soon shaken in mind or troubled, either by spirit or by word or by letter, as if from us, as though the day of Christ had come. 3 Let no one deceive you by any means; for that Day will not come unless the falling away comes first, and the man of sin is revealed, the son of perdition, 4 who opposes and exalts himself above all that is called God or that is worshiped, so that he sits as God in the temple of God, showing himself that he is God. 5 Do you not remember that when I was still with you I told you these things? 6 And now you know what is restraining, that he may be revealed in his own time. 7 For the mystery of lawlessness is already at work; only He who now restrains will do so until He is taken out of the way. 8 And then the lawless one will be revealed, whom the Lord will consume with the breath of His mouth and destroy with the brightness of His coming.

Those that choose to agree with Jesus, that choose to live LIKE Him, will live close to Him, forever. That brings us to the reward. The reward for overcoming, staying steady in using David's Key, in agreement with God will bringing the Bride closer and closer to the throne. If you choose to build the temple worship on earth, you will inhabit the temple, the "whIte house" of Jesus' government, forever:

4. *Revelation 3:12 He who overcomes, I will make him a pillar in the temple of My God, and he shall go out no more. I will write on him the name of My God and the name of the city of My God, the New Jerusalem, which comes down out of heaven from My God. And I will write on him My new name.*

This IS Jesus' plan to overcome evil and drive it off the planet. Jesus' partner, His co-heir, must agree that this is true, yet seemingly weak, strength. The opening of heaven, the releasing of glory, and the singing of truth that matches what heaven is singing IS THE ONLY PLAN TO DEFEAT DARKNESS. Jesus said it will surely work, but then He asked the most chilling question: How many will Jesus find that have enough faith to cry out night and day that He is the good leader of the earth, when He allows the enemy armies to have the evil desire in their heart? When He brings vengeance, it will be to those praying night and day:

Luke 18:7-8 And shall God not _avenge_ His own elect who cry _out day and night to Him_, though He bears long with them? 8 I tell you that He will avenge them speedily. Nevertheless, _when the Son of Man comes, will He really find faith on the earth?_"

He who has an ear, let him hear what the Spirit says to the churches.

Chapter 8 - Laodicea

"Lukewarm"

Revelation 3:14-22 "And to the angel of the church of the Laodiceans write, 'These things says the Amen, the Faithful and True Witness, the Beginning of the creation of God: 15 "I know your works, that you are neither cold nor hot. I could wish you were cold or hot. 16 So then, because you are lukewarm, and neither cold nor hot, I will vomit you out of My mouth. 17 Because you say, 'I am rich, have become wealthy, and have need of nothing'—and do not know that you are wretched, miserable, poor, blind, and naked— 18 I counsel you to buy from Me gold refined in the fire, that you may be rich; and white garments, that you may be clothed, that the shame of your nakedness may not be revealed; and anoint your eyes with eye salve, that you may see. 19 As many as I love, I rebuke and chasten. Therefore be zealous and repent. 20 Behold, I stand at the door and knock. If anyone hears My voice and opens the door, I will come in to him and dine with him, and he with Me. 21 To him who overcomes I will grant to sit with Me on My throne, as I also overcame and sat down with My Father on His throne. 22 "He who has an ear, let him hear what the Spirit says to the churches." ' "

Earthly comfort is the problem the hour we live in. I know this is an unpopular message, but according to the Bible, earthly comfort is the last thing you are supposed to be trying to build in your life.

Matthew 16:24-26 Then Jesus said to His disciples, "If anyone desires to come after Me, let him deny himself, and take up his cross, and follow Me. 25 For whoever desires to save his life will lose it, but whoever loses his life for My sake will find it. 26 For what profit is it to a man if he gains the whole world, and loses his own soul? Or what will a man give in exchange for his soul?

Laodicea has missed this essential truth of the Gospel of Jesus. There is only one Gospel and the hour that Laodicea is about to enter into will reveal that she does not have the true Gospel, the one that actually works.

The events described in the Book of Revelation are describing the maturing of the age, or the end of the harvest. That means what has been true for centuries will be shown to be more true as the growing season comes to harvest. What has always been false will be shown to be more false, as the growing season comes to harvest. Let's look at the four-fold pattern for the last of the seven churches and see what the Spirit is saying to us in this hour:

1. Jesus addresses Laodicea with a three-fold identity as "the Amen, the Faithful and True Witness, the Beginning of the creation of God"

The Amen: Jesus is saying He is the one who AGREED with the Father about what REAL life is. Jesus did what Adam failed to do: live in perfect trust and obedience to the Father's leadership, no matter how troubling that leadership looked:

Mark 14:36 And He said, "Abba, Father, all things are possible for You. Take this cup away from Me; nevertheless, not what I will, but what You will."

By obeying the Father even to his own natural death, Jesus beat death. This brings us to His second chosen identity: The Faithful and True witness.

By being the "Amen" to the Father and agreeing with God that real life WITH Him was worth the immediate cost of a sacrificed life without Him face to face, Jesus beat death. He said that all who wanted to share in the defeat of death should take up their cross and follow Him. By His own success, Jesus proved that it is this true Gospel of sharing in His sacrifice that will bring greatness to all mankind humble enough to accept it. Jesus is the Faithful and True witness about where real life happens: face to face with God, on earth, forever.

Laodicea thinks life is already happening. Because of her unusual comfort, Laodicea mistakenly believes life outside of God's ultimate desire of being face to face with His people is really good. Jesus has already proven that He does not agree with Laodicea. Jesus wasted his natural life because He was looking forward to the Father's desire for very good. Because He humbled Himself to agree with the Father's desire, He will rule over the kings of the earth:

Philippians 2:5-10 Let this mind be in you which was also in Christ Jesus, 6 who, being in the form of God, did not consider it robbery to be equal with God, 7 but made Himself of no reputation, taking the form of a bondservant, and coming in the likeness of men. 8 And being found in appearance as a man, He humbled Himself and became obedient to the point of death, even the death of the cross. 9 Therefore God also has highly exalted Him and given Him the name which is above every name, 10 that at the name of Jesus every knee should bow, of those in heaven, and of those on earth, and of those under the earth,

This is part of Jesus' identity as the Faithful Witness:

Revelation 1:5 and from Jesus Christ, the faithful witness, the firstborn from the dead, and the ruler over the kings of the earth. To Him who loved us and washed us from our sins in His own blood,

The third identity is the most powerful one to understand: The Beginning of the creation of God.

Jesus is saying that He is the SOURCE of life. By calling Himself this, He is proclaiming that if you don't agree with him ("Amen" with Him) about His Faithful Witnessing of Truth, then you do not really want true life with Him. This is all about self denial now, so that life can begin when Jesus comes back and restores what He made in Genesis 1.

John 1:2-7 He was in the beginning with God. 3 All things were made through Him, and without Him nothing was made that was made. 4 In Him was life, and the life was the light of men. 5 And the light shines in the darkness, and the darkness did not comprehend it. 6 There was a man sent from God, whose name was John. 7 This man came for a witness, to bear witness of the Light, that all through him might believe.

John the Baptist was the forerunner of self-denial. Have you ever wondered why God chose John the Baptist to make the way before Jesus? What does that mean? To understand this, you have to consider: How did John live?

Matthew 3:1-7 In those days John the Baptist came preaching in the wilderness of Judea, 2 and saying, "Repent, for the kingdom of heaven is at hand!" 3 For this is he who was spoken of by the prophet Isaiah, saying: "THE VOICE OF ONE CRYING IN THE WILDERNESS: 'PREPARE THE WAY OF THE LORD; MAKE HIS PATHS STRAIGHT.' " 4 Now John himself was clothed in camel's hair, with a leather belt around his waist; and his food was locusts and wild honey. 5 Then Jerusalem, all Judea, and all the region around the Jordan went out to him 6 and were baptized by him in the Jordan, confessing their sins. 7 But when he saw many of the Pharisees and Sadducees coming to his baptism, he said to them, "Brood of vipers! Who warned you to flee from the wrath to come?

Denial of self, which is separation from the comfort the world is trying to live in, and an "all-in" participation with Jesus in His return has always been the true response of a follower of Jesus. That is what John did first, before anyone else. This is the spiritual violence that John the Baptist started 2,000 years ago. Jesus agreed with it. Jesus, the King of Kings, came and lived the same way as John. Jesus was the Amen to the Truth that life is only really possible when the Father comes back into the Garden. Until that day, John and Jesus chose to contend for that to happen with everything they had. They did not want a good life apart from the Father coming home. This is a violent separation from what the world values. Violent separation on the inside of our hearts from the worlds false value system is what will tear the veil between earth and heaven. This is how the kingdom will come: by spiritual violence! Jesus knows this is an offensive message. He told John's disciples to guard against being offended by this message:

Matthew 11:6-15 And blessed is he who is not offended because of Me." 7 As they departed, Jesus began to say to the multitudes concerning John: "What did you go out into the wilderness to see? A reed shaken by the wind? 8 But what did you go out to see? A man clothed in soft garments? Indeed, those who wear soft clothing are in kings' houses. 9 But what did you go out to see? A prophet? Yes, I say to you, and more than a prophet. 10 For this is he of whom it is written: 'BEHOLD, I SEND MY MESSENGER BEFORE YOUR FACE, WHO WILL PREPARE YOUR WAY BEFORE YOU.' 11 "Assuredly, I say to you, among those born of women there has not risen one greater than John the Baptist; but he who is least in the kingdom of heaven is greater than he. 12 And from the days of John the Baptist until now the kingdom of heaven suffers violence, and the violent take it by force. 13 For all the prophets and the law prophesied until John. 14 And if you are willing to receive it, he is Elijah who is to come. 15 He who has ears to hear, let him hear!

This is important to understand, and sadly, many pastors and teachers will never teach you this. Even in John's day, the paid spokespeople for God resisted this message in John's life, and eventually killed Jesus. The paid leaders in the churches often don't like this message, because if they preach it, they are obligated to try to live it. That is why John said this to the Pharisees and Sadducees:

Matthew 3:7 But when he saw many of the Pharisees and Sadducees coming to his baptism, he said to them, "Brood of vipers! Who warned you to flee from the wrath to come?

According to the Bible, there are many false "leaders" in the end-time church, those who have made their job representing God to "the people." According to Jesus, many of these people are actually IN the church seeming to do amazing things. They cast out demons, they prophesy, they heal people, and they do it all to make a name for themselves. They have simply found an interesting career path, a place to feel important, or they religiously think God will approve of them because they have dedicated their "livelihood" to him. God doesn't want to be your job, He wants to be your everything, your very life, whether you work for Him or not. He cares more about the secret motivation of your heart than He does the outward appearance of love. These false teachers, and the ones who follow them, have missed the most basic Genesis 1 fact: there is no life possible apart from face to face contact with the life-source of mankind. This is where God is leading the Bride. If the leaders aren't heading here, too, they are leading in lawlessness:

Matthew 7:21-23 "Not everyone who says to Me, 'Lord, Lord,' shall enter the kingdom of heaven, but he who does the will of My Father in heaven. 22 Many will say to Me in that day, 'Lord, Lord, have we not prophesied in Your name, cast out demons in Your name, and done many wonders in Your name?' 23 And then I will declare to them, 'I never knew you; depart from Me, you who practice lawlessness!'

Just like in John the Baptist's day, these false leaders do not want you zealously trading your life for this all in desire to do everything you can. Many leaders don't want you to get too zealous in fasting, praying, teaching the negative aspects of the end time truth to warn people, giving your money away, and denying yourself, because if you, the lowly people, do it, then they have to do it more, since they have claimed to be your "leaders."

According to Jesus, these leaders are serving God because it is their profession, not their only hope and desire. They are hired hands who are deadly to the Church in a time of trouble:

John 10:11-13 "I am the good shepherd. The good shepherd gives His life for the sheep. 12 But a hireling, he who is not the shepherd, one who does not own the sheep, sees the wolf coming and leaves the sheep and flees; and the wolf catches the sheep and scatters them. 13 The hireling flees because he is a hireling and does not care about the sheep.

There are many good under shepherds who lead others in wholehearted love for Jesus, but there are also many hired hands. You have to be discerning and watch for the hired hands. This is Laodicea's main problem: those who claim to be the true knower's of God have never encouraged her about the true gospel, just like in the time of Jesus' appearing, those who claimed to know wouldn't enter in, and actually prevented others from going in to true life:

Matthew 23:11-13 The greatest among you must be a servant. 12 But those who exalt themselves will be humbled, and those who humble themselves will be exalted. 13 "What sorrow awaits you teachers of religious law and you Pharisees. Hypocrites! For you shut the door of the Kingdom of Heaven in people's faces. You won't go in yourselves, and you don't let others enter either.

True leaders agree with Jesus about giving their lives in self denial that they might be a living example of what it looks like to walk through the door and follow the Way, the Truth, and the Life. If a hired hand has to go do something for God's people outside of their job description, they take time off of their regular day. The hired hand wants to make sure he has a good role to fill at the meeting or even, or he probably won't show up. The hired hand hangs with the other managers, but won't actually do the common "stuff" unless everyone is watching. The true Bride works her job all day then goes joyfully to serve and worship, and she doesn't care if anyone knows it. She can't wait to be a part of the return of Jesus, any part, because she is lovesick! She just wants Jesus back in the Garden, even if it means the Great Tribulation.

The hired hands, those false prophets, teachers, and shepherds, simply expect to be compensated for their love either monetarily, through increasing honor, or through the praise of the people. False leaders in the church are not the "Amen" to Jesus, they are the Amen to the Harlot Babylon, who does what the Bride is supposed to do, only for pay instead of covenant love.

Church workers should get paid, really good ones should get paid double, but then, like everyone else, their passion, paid or not, should be to do as much as possible to find out what Jesus' plans are and then spend themselves on those plans, while denying themselves in a way that makes them different from the rest of the world. The Bride, whether she is employed by the church or not, is willing to forgo life now until the Groom returns:

Matthew 9:15 And Jesus said to them, "Can the friends of the bridegroom mourn as long as the bridegroom is with them? But the days will come when the bridegroom will be taken away from them, and then they will fast.

This is how the first disciples, and the vast majority of the early church, lived. They lived this way largely because the true leaders were continually pointing them to the fact that our entire lives are to be about Jesus coming back:

1 John 2:18 Little children, it is the last hour; and as you have heard that the Antichrist is coming, even now many antichrists have come, by which we know that it is the last hour.

2 Peter 3:10-12 But the day of the Lord will come as a thief in the night, in which the heavens will pass away with a great noise, and the elements will melt with fervent heat; both the earth and the works that are in it will be burned up. 11 Therefore, since all these things will be dissolved, <u>what manner of persons ought you to be in holy conduct and godliness, 12 looking for and hastening the coming of the day of God</u>, because of which the heavens will be dissolved, being on fire, and the elements will melt with fervent heat?

Laodicea does not want to be that "manner of person." She wants to love Jesus AND her comfy life. She thinks "Isn't that what God would want? He didn't create ME to suffer tribulation or to deny myself, right?" To believe this line of thinking is to believe the Tribulation lifestyle was just for God's son and His best friends!

The truth is, Laodicea doesn't believe in violently separating from the world. She believes in balance, lukewarm, and comfort. Laodicea's love for her life now makes Jesus feel sick to His stomach! That brings us to the correction:

2. *Revelation 3:15 "I know your works, that you are neither cold nor hot. I could wish you were cold or hot. 16 So then, because you are lukewarm, and neither cold nor hot, I will vomit you out of My mouth. 17 Because you say, 'I am rich, have become*

> *wealthy, and have need of nothing'—and do not know that you*
> *are wretched, miserable, poor, blind, and naked—*

Laodicea has no vision for what is coming, so she is completely unprepared to endure the Tribulation, this makes Jesus sick to His stomach. He sees the Tribulation coming at his beloved like a freight train and knows she can't possibly live through what is coming without changing. All of her strength is in worldly success. But, Jesus is going to strip away every man-based strength from the earth to judge the false strength of the world. Jesus is going to prove to the earth that they can not live without God in the Garden! You cannot live apart from the source of life, and Jesus is going to prove that to the earth over the course of 7 years by pouring out more life on the people that say "amen" to the Amen, and by stripping life from those who refuse to humble themselves and say Amen to God's definition of life! By their lives and letters all the first leaders clearly believed this. Laodicea has been deceived by her later leaders.

We are actually, by the clear signs of prophetic fulfillment, in the last hour. Earthly comfort is being swept out of the land by Jesus, on purpose. Have you looked around lately? This isn't rocket science. The only reason some of us can still buy Audi's and TV's is because our government is falsely propping up our economy. Our government is trying to keep the hand of God at bay. It will come crashing down...soon. You cannot wrestle Jesus and win.

Let me say this clearly: by the simple political movements the Bible describes in Daniel 7 and Daniel 11, we are clearly in the hour Daniel was told would lead to the Tribulation. Those very specific political signs have never happened before. Additionally, the aligning of the Muslim Brotherhood with the American administration sparked the greatest increase in persecution of Christians our generation has ever seen. This all began with the Arab Spring on December 19, 2010. By the prophecy in Revelation 2 over Smyrna, where Jesus promised she would enter into tribulation 3 years before the rest of the world, I personally believe the 7-year Tribulation has, in fact, started as of December 2013, three years after the Arab Spring began setting the Middle East on fire.

The facts on the ground in the Middle East, and elsewhere, support me in this observation. A revival of the Ottoman Empire, which is the seventh empire of Revelation 17, called a caliphate, has emerged. Israel is in a corner and the United States are the ones backing her into it. Hamas (the Muslim Brotherhood) is enjoying great negative influence in Israel with our money and political support. Let me tell you clearly what the Bible says is coming next:

Matthew 24:9-14 "Then they will deliver you up to tribulation and kill you, and you will be hated by all nations for My name's sake. 10 And then many will be offended, will betray one another, and will hate one another. 11 Then many false prophets will rise up and deceive many. 12 And because lawlessness will abound, the love of many will grow cold. 13 But he who endures to the end shall be saved. 14 And this gospel of the kingdom will be preached in all the world as a witness to all the nations, and then the end will come.

Believing that Jesus wants you to carve out a nice place for yourself and add Him to your cute life is a lie, and worse, it won't work in this hour. This is Laodicea's problem, she has things backwards. She wants to put her trust in the stuff so she can praise Jesus. Jesus wants her to put her trust in Him so the stuff doesn't hold her hostage!

Laodicea does not understand the basic principal of true life: Jesus wants back into the Father's garden so He can begin preparing it to live again in the light of the Father. Jesus' Bride is supposed to long for this to happen so much that she is ruined for anything less. If she does this, seeks His kingdom with everything first, then she will have whatever else she needs no matter who is in control of the resources.

Because Jesus loves, He will not force His Bride to get ready. Instead, Jesus has a brilliant plan to get His self-focused and divided Bride to actually wake up and cast off the warm blanket of earthly comfort. Jesus has promised to do this by commanding the wind and waves to storm around her. Jesus is allowing a storm to form to pull away all false comfort so that there is only one true desire left standing. This is what Jesus did with His best friends! He let a storm rise up so they would call on Him (Mark 4:39). He is going to do this one last time globally. Everyone who agrees with truth in the end will cry out day and night: GOD, PLEASE COME BACK SO I CAN LIVE!

This means that Jesus is removing His hand of restraint from the evil desires in men's hearts in order to make the world a very stormy place. Faith in Jesus, which is true comfort for storms, is what we are supposed to be acquiring because we will need it now, and because we will enjoy it forever. That is why the faithful counselor is counseling us to change our value system:

> 3.   *I counsel you to buy from Me gold refined in the fire, that you may be rich; and white garments, that you may be clothed, that the shame of your nakedness may not be revealed; and anoint your eyes with eye salve, that you may see. 19 As many as I love, I rebuke and chasten. Therefore be zealous and repent.*

Like any good Father, God wants His children to live for what is coming so they are prepared. Like foolish children, many in the western church have stopped caring much about what dad is warning about, and instead have begun twisting the Father's true principles to make them more about living in the moment.

The end time Tribulation is about entirely disrupting the comfort that the fallen earth has turned her gaze to. God is going to remove every comfort most of the USA has come to think is required, and, even worse, taught the world to value. God is actually planning to remove your false comfort, and mine! The false comforts of our day and age that have tricked us into believing that life without God is pretty good include 401k's, savings accounts, checking balance, wine, fancy clothes, vacations, trucks, cars, career status, social status, and many other trappings of western civilization. God is going to pull away these distractions on purpose, so that we will let go of a lie and embrace truth. This is promised to be global. Look who claims responsibility for the devastation:

Isaiah 24:1-15 Behold, the LORD makes the earth empty and makes it waste, Distorts its surface And scatters abroad its inhabitants. 2 And it shall be: As with the people, so with the priest; As with the servant, so with his master; As with the maid, so with her mistress; As with the buyer, so with the seller; As with the lender, so with the borrower; As with the creditor, so with the debtor. 3 The land shall be entirely emptied and utterly plundered, For the LORD has spoken this word. 4 The earth mourns and fades away, The world languishes and fades away; The haughty people of the earth languish. 5 The earth is also defiled under its inhabitants, Because they have transgressed the laws, Changed the ordinance, Broken the everlasting covenant. 6 Therefore the curse has devoured the earth, And those who dwell in it are desolate. Therefore the inhabitants of the earth are burned, And few men are left. 7 The new wine fails, the vine languishes, All the merry-hearted sigh. 8 The mirth of the tambourine ceases, The noise of the jubilant ends, The joy of the harp ceases. 9 They shall not drink wine with a song; Strong drink is bitter to those who drink it. 10 The city of confusion is broken down; Every house is shut up, so that none may go in. 11 There is a cry for wine in the streets, All joy is darkened, The mirth of the land is gone. 12 In the city desolation is left, And the gate is stricken with destruction. 13 When it shall be thus in the midst of the land among the people, It shall be like the shaking of an olive tree, Like the gleaning of grapes when the vintage is done. 14 They shall lift up their voice, they shall sing; For the majesty of the LORD They shall cry aloud from the sea. 15 Therefore glorify the LORD in the dawning light, The name of the LORD God of Israel in the coastlands of the sea.

Do you see the last two verses? Do you see that there will be a people SINGING about the removal of comfort? Those loyal to Jesus will agree that the false comfort is actually killing the people Jesus loves. This is because the earth is mostly asleep to the fact that what they are calling life is much less than what God called very good in Genesis 1:31. The Great Tribulation is the final stage in preparing the earth for the restoration of Genesis 1:31. This is a very intense plan.

To get ready to endure this plan, Laodicea is counseled to BUY some things. That means they cost. Each of the items Jesus instructs Laodicea she will need to overcome the Tribulation are things purchased by living the Sermon on the Mount. Trading the cheap and dying earthly comforts for true wealth that will not only comfort her through the events of the Tribulation, but will last for eternity as true luxury.   As Jesus has told all seven churches in different ways: holiness is what matters. And Laodicea, like all the other churches, needs to make herself ready for the wedding.

The Sermon on the Mount is the roadmap to holiness. The Sermon on the Mount (Matthew 5, 6, and 7) is the most straight-forward, clear, and comprehensive statement of how to obey the Gospel and follow Jesus. It starts with humility in recognizing what you lack compared to Jesus and mourning it, and ends with the end time return of Jesus to judge everyone, first in the Church, who doesn't agree with His faithful witness that we are supposed to be living for the next age. The fire is going to test everyone to see if they have really loved Jesus wholeheartedly, as He loves them. Love is evidenced by obedience!

1 Peter 4:16-19 Yet if anyone suffers as a Christian, let him not be ashamed, but let him glorify God in this matter. 17 For the time has come for judgment to begin at the house of God; and if it begins with us first, what will be the end of those who do not obey the gospel of God? 18 Now "IF THE RIGHTEOUS ONE IS SCARCELY SAVED, WHERE WILL THE UNGODLY AND THE SINNER APPEAR?" 19 Therefore let those who suffer according to the will of God commit their souls to Him in doing good, as to a faithful Creator.

Let's look at what Jesus counsels Laodicea to acquire in advance of the Great Tribulation:

a.   Gold refined in fire. The "Sermon on the Mount Mart" has this kind of gold. This is how you buy it:

Matthew 6:19-21 "Do not lay up for yourselves treasures on earth, where moth and rust destroy and where thieves break in and steal; 20 but lay up for yourselves treasures in heaven, where neither moth nor rust destroys and where thieves do not break in and steal. 21 For where your treasure is, there your heart will be also.

The true treasure that lasts forever is purchased through the fire of testing. This isn't talking about just giving your 10% tithe and considering the rest of your money yours!. This is talking about extravagant, irresponsible by American standards, generosity. This is talking about taking what you are planning to retire on and using it, as other people's needs arise, to help them. Giving just to get free of the grip of money on your own heart. How much should you give? Enough to make it hurt. This is what frees you from the snare of money. You have to do it secretly, so that the only reward is freedom from the money itself. Many will give out of their abundance, but few will give what they are actually planning to live on:

Mark 12:41-44 Now Jesus sat opposite the treasury and saw how the people put money into the treasury. And many who were rich put in much. 42 Then one poor widow came and threw in two mites, which make a quadrans. 43 So He called His disciples to Himself and said to them, "Assuredly, I say to you that this poor widow has put in more than all those who have given to the treasury; 44 for they all put in out of their abundance, but she out of her poverty put in all that she had, her whole livelihood."

If you think God is mostly concerned about you having a responsible and solid retirement over trusting that He is your trillion-year retirement plan and can provide for you no matter what, you absolutely do not know Him in the area of your money. This is almost NEVER preached in the American church, but this is a significant part of the Gospel. If you don't believe this, then you do not believe the Good News that Jesus has paid for you to live forever with Him on a renewed earth and how you hold your money now will forever affect the quality of your life with Him forever.

Luke 12:16-26 Then He spoke a parable to them, saying: "The ground of a certain rich man yielded plentifully. 17 And he thought within himself, saying, 'What shall I do, since I have no room to store my crops?' 18 So he said, 'I will do this: I will pull down my barns and build greater, and there I will store all my crops and my goods. 19 And I will say to my soul, "Soul, you have many goods laid up for many years; take your ease; eat, drink, and be merry." ' 20 But God said to him, 'Fool! This night your soul will be required of you; then whose will those things be which you have provided?' 21 "So is he who lays up treasure for himself, and is not rich toward God." 22 Then He said to His disciples, "Therefore I say to you, do not worry about your life, what you will eat; nor about the body, what you will put on. 23 Life is more than food, and the body is more than clothing. 24 Consider the ravens, for they neither sow nor reap, which have neither storehouse nor barn; and God feeds them. Of how much more value are you than the birds? 25 And which of you by worrying can add one cubit to his stature? 26 If you then are not able to do the least, why are you anxious for the rest?

Only in the last 150 years was the concept of a "retirement" even imagined, and then, only in the industrialized western world. This concept of saving for a time when you would live on that wealth for any length of time would be foreign to 99.9% of the people to HAVE EVER INHABITED PLANET EARTH, yet many western churches actually preach that God wants you to be a good saver. This is a deceit.

The antichrist is going to confiscate the savings of every believer. Right now in Iraq and Syria, believers are already having their wealth confiscated if they stay loyal to Jesus. This is going global, and if you do not prepare now, your moth-prone dollars and cents will be the very thing that entices you to compromise with the antichrist and take his mark so you can keep working and not "lose it all." One way or the other you must lose it all, either by denying yourself and taking up your cross voluntarily now, or having your wealth confiscated in the last 3.5 years. If you die to it now, it cannot kill you later. If aren't willing to die to your wealth now, what will you do then, when the antichrist threatens your existence with the same wealth?:

Revelation 13:16-17 He causes all, both small and great, rich and poor, free and slave, to receive a mark on their right hand or on their foreheads, 17 and that no one may buy or sell except one who has the mark or the name of the beast, or the number of his name.

No one who takes the mark can live. You will forever burn in a lake of fire if you choose to keep access to your money. This is what Jesus is sick to His stomach about fixing in the heart of Laodicea:

Revelation 14:11 And the smoke of their torment ascends forever and ever; and they have no rest day or night, who worship the beast and his image, and whoever receives the mark of his name."

    b.   Jesus also tells Laodicea to buy "white garments to hide your nakedness." Again, these garments are found in aisle 6 of "Sermon On the Mount Mart":

Matthew 6:28-33 "So why do you worry about clothing? Consider the lilies of the field, how they grow: they neither toil nor spin; 29 and yet I say to you that even Solomon in all his glory was not arrayed like one of these. 30 Now if God so clothes the grass of the field, which today is, and tomorrow is thrown into the oven, will He not much more clothe you, O you of little faith? 31 "Therefore do not worry, saying, 'What shall we eat?' or 'What shall we drink?' or 'What shall we wear?' 32 For after all these things the Gentiles seek. For your heavenly Father knows that you need all these things. 33 But seek first the kingdom of God and His righteousness, and all these things shall be added to you.

If you do not buy these garments, you simply WILL NOT MARRY JESUS:

Matthew 22:10-13 So those servants went out into the highways and gathered together all whom they found, both bad and good. And the wedding hall was filled with guests. 11 "But when the king came in to see the guests, he saw a man there who did not have on a wedding garment. 12 So he said to him, 'Friend, how did you come in here without a wedding garment?' And he was speechless. 13 Then the king said to the servants, 'Bind him hand and foot, take him away, and cast him into outer darkness; there will be weeping and gnashing of teeth.'

Just to be clear, the Bible tells us the Bride gets herself ready, by growing in holiness, through the Sermon on the Mount. This isn't tricky theology or sleight of hand with Bible verses, just the main and plain meaning of the Bible. This is what wedding garments are:

Revelation 19:7-8 Let us be glad and rejoice and give Him glory, for the marriage of the Lamb has come, and His wife has made herself ready." 8 And to her it was granted to be arrayed in fine linen, clean and bright, for the fine linen is the righteous acts of the saints.

    c.   Jesus also tells Laodicea to buy "eye salve." She needs healed eyes which will give her a new vision of life that goes past the 70 or 80 years she thinks is life. If you don't see life as beginning in Genesis 1:31, stopping in Genesis 3, and not starting again until Revelation 19, then you have a bad eye. You need salve. Know where to buy it? That's right! "Mountain Mart:"

Matthew 6:22-24 "The lamp of the body is the eye. If therefore your eye is good, your whole body will be full of light. 23 But if your eye is bad, your whole body will be full of darkness. If therefore the light that is in you is darkness, how great is that darkness! 24 "No one can serve two masters; for either he will hate the one and love the other, or else he will be loyal to the one and despise the other. You cannot serve God and mammon.

Denying yourself now and living for the time when Jesus returns to earth is "Christianity 101." There is no other Gospel. The problem Laodicea has is related to where she lives. Laodicea is a western mindset. Because of the American experience, many globally want comfort, and the west has it. In fact, our lust for comfort is one of the reasons God judges end time Babylon.

Let me say this plainly: I believe we live in the end time Babylon. Almost every church in the western world has a touch of the Laodicea fever, and some are actually consumed by it, as health and wealth now, before Jesus returns, has become their very theology. Revelation 18 describes what the Great Tribulation is going to do to the end time Babylon, and why. Listen, if this isn't describing America, how does this passage indicate God feels about the America we know?:

Revelation 18:1-24 After these things I saw another angel coming down from heaven, having great authority, and the earth was illuminated with his glory. 2 And he cried mightily with a loud voice, saying, "Babylon the great is fallen, is fallen, and has become a dwelling place of demons, a prison for every foul spirit, and a cage for every unclean and hated bird! 3 For all the nations have drunk of the wine of the wrath of her fornication, the kings of the earth have committed fornication with her, and the merchants of the earth have become rich through the abundance of her luxury." 4 And I heard another voice from heaven saying, "Come out of her, my people, lest you share in her sins, and lest you receive of her plagues. 5 For her sins have reached to heaven, and God has remembered her iniquities. 6 Render to her just as she rendered to you, and repay her double according to her works; in the cup which she has mixed, mix double for her. 7 In the measure that she glorified herself and lived luxuriously, in the same measure give her torment and sorrow; for she says in her heart, 'I sit as queen, and am no widow, and will not see sorrow.' 8 Therefore her plagues will come in one day—death and mourning and famine. And she will be utterly burned with fire, for strong is the Lord God who judges her. 9 "The kings of the earth who committed fornication and lived luxuriously with her will weep and lament for her, when they see the smoke of her burning, 10 standing at a distance for fear of her torment, saying, 'Alas, alas, that great city Babylon, that mighty city! For in one hour your judgment has come.' 11 "And the merchants of the earth will weep and mourn over her, for no one buys their merchandise anymore: 12 merchandise of gold and silver, precious stones and pearls, fine linen and purple, silk and scarlet, every kind of citron wood, every kind of object of ivory, every kind of object of most precious wood, bronze, iron, and marble; 13 and cinnamon and incense, fragrant oil and frankincense, wine and oil, fine flour and wheat, cattle and sheep, horses and chariots, and bodies and souls of men. 14 The fruit that your soul longed for has gone from you, and all the things which are rich and splendid have gone from you, and you shall find them no more at all. 15 The merchants of these things, who became rich by her, will stand at a distance for fear of her torment, weeping and wailing, 16 and saying, 'Alas, alas, that great city that was clothed in fine linen, purple, and scarlet, and adorned with gold and precious stones and pearls! 17 For in one hour such great riches came to nothing.' Every shipmaster, all who travel by ship, sailors, and as many as trade on the sea, stood at a distance 18 and cried out when they saw the smoke of her burning, saying, 'What is like this great city?' 19 "They threw dust on their heads and cried out, weeping and wailing, and saying, 'Alas, alas, that great city, in which all who had ships on the sea became rich by her wealth! For in one hour she is made desolate.' 20 "Rejoice over her, O heaven, and you holy apostles and prophets, for God has avenged you on her!" 21 Then a mighty angel took up a stone like a great millstone and threw it into the sea, saying, "Thus with violence the great city Babylon shall be thrown down, and shall not be found anymore. 22 The sound of harpists, musicians, flutists, and trumpeters shall not be heard in you anymore. No craftsman of any craft shall be found in you anymore, and the sound of a millstone shall not be heard in you anymore. 23 The light of a lamp shall not shine in you anymore, and the voice of bridegroom and bride shall not be heard in you anymore. For your merchants were the great men of the earth, for by your sorcery all the nations were deceived. 24 And in her was found the blood of prophets and saints, and of all who were slain on the earth."

Everyone must overcome the luxury of the land they were born into. This isn't just for the "rich." Many of those who have relatively little are plagued with the hunger to taste the same things "everyone else has" (that is a lie, you know. 90% of the world is lusting for even less than you have if you are an American). If you don't overcome what seems normal to Americans, you will suffer the same fate described in Revelation 18, by your own choice.

Anyone can "come out" of Babylon. If you choose to stay in her, you will not have what it takes to make it through what is clearly coming. That is why, according to Jesus, Laodicea is poor, wretched, blind, and naked. They simply don't have the true Gospel to endure the time of testing. Laodicea is flat broke and doesn't know it because they won't let go of the worthless wealth and dreams they are holding instead of the dream of Jesus' heart. Jesus' dream for you is very good, it is God with man in the garden. If Laodicea had that dream in her eye, she would gladly trade every last cent and every last minute to hasten the day of Jesus' return. If Laodicea shared the Groom's vision, she would be red hot on fire for Jesus to return. She needs to answer the knock at the door to overcome.

Oh, to overcome is life! The promise for Laodicea is the grandest of all. You see, the richer you are, the harder it is to be saved, but when you lay down great wealth, you are more like Jesus. Jesus had it all, and laid it all down:

Philippians 2:4-9 Don't look out only for your own interests, but take an interest in others, too. 5 You must have the same attitude that Christ Jesus had. 6 Though He was God, He did not think of equality with God as something to cling to. 7 Instead, He gave up His divine privileges; He took the humble position of a slave and was born as a human being. When He appeared in human form, 8 He humbled Himself in obedience to God and died a criminal's death on a cross. 9 Therefore, God elevated Him to the place of highest honor and gave Him the name above all other names,

That brings us to part four of the pattern, the reward for casting off false comfort:

4. *Revelation 3:20 Behold, I stand at the door and knock. If anyone hears My voice and opens the door, I will come in to him and dine with him, and he with Me. 21 To him who overcomes I will*

grant to sit with Me on My throne, as I also overcame and sat
down with My Father on His throne.

Jesus LOVES Laodicea. He knows how hard it is to come out of comfort, because He left perfect comfort for her! If she is willing to come out and be the "Amen" to God's economy, and the "faithful witness" to the fact that Jesus tells the truth, if she is willing to actually believe that life doesn't begin until He is back on the planet, then Jesus will give her the right to rule with Him forever. This is the pinnacle of rewards. This is the same thing He offered to the rich young ruler. This wealthy young man could have been one of the 12 disciples, ruling on 12 thrones forever:

Matthew 19:20-28 "I've obeyed all these commandments," the young man replied. "What else must I do?" 21 Jesus told him, "If you want to be perfect, go and sell all your possessions and give the money to the poor, and you will have treasure in heaven. Then come, follow Me." 22 But when the young man heard this, he went away sad, for he had many possessions. 23 Then Jesus said to His disciples, "I tell you the truth, it is very hard for a rich person to enter the Kingdom of Heaven. 24 I'll say it again—it is easier for a camel to go through the eye of a needle than for a rich person to enter the Kingdom of God!" 25 The disciples were astounded. "Then who in the world can be saved?" they asked. 26 Jesus looked at them intently and said, "Humanly speaking, it is impossible. But with God everything is possible." 27 Then Peter said to Him, "We've given up everything to follow You. What will we get?" 28 Jesus replied, "I assure you that when the world is made new and the Son of Man sits upon His glorious throne, you who have been My followers will also sit on twelve thrones, judging the twelve tribes of Israel.

This is impossible for man, but with God, everything is possible. That is why the Tribulation, and the Great Tribulation, must come. All the false comfort is going so that there is only one true desire left standing. This is what all the world is supposed to be demanding from heaven: GOD, PLEASE COME BACK SO I CAN LIVE!

If God removed the air from the earth, we would all suddenly only care about air. We know we need air to live. This is how we are all supposed to feel about Jesus. If we really understood the truth of life, the entire earth would be on a non-stop protest to heaven...night and day...until God gave us back Himself, or we died.

Right now, in this hour, God is shining the light of truth on the darkness in men's hearts. That is why the earth is increasing in intensity...murder, theft, acts of war. The only solution is for the source of life to come back to the garden. As people wake up to this truth in humility, they will begin a 24-hour cry out to God to come back, and He will:

Luke 18:1-8 Then He spoke a parable to them, that men always ought to pray and not lose heart, 2 saying: "There was in a certain city a judge who did not fear God nor regard man. 3 Now there was a widow in that city; and she came to him, saying, 'Get justice for me from my adversary.' 4 And he would not for a while; but afterward he said within himself, 'Though I do not fear God nor regard man, 5 yet because this widow troubles me I will avenge her, lest by her continual coming she weary me.' " 6 Then the Lord said, "Hear what the unjust judge said. 7 And shall God not avenge His own elect who cry out day and night to Him, though He bears long with them? 8 I tell you that He will avenge them speedily. Nevertheless, when the Son of Man comes, will He really find faith on the earth?"

He who has an ear, let him hear what the Spirit says to the churches

Chapter 9 – Contending With Jesus

Jesus wants back on earth. He is contending for US to be ready. All of creation is not groaning for a new president, or less carbon emissions, or clean water in Africa...NO! All of creation is groaning for this:

Romans 8:19-22 For the earnest expectation of the creation eagerly waits for the revealing of the sons of God. 20 For the creation was subjected to futility, not willingly, but because of Him who subjected it in hope; 21 because the creation itself also will be delivered from the bondage of corruption into the glorious liberty of the children of God. 22 For we know that the whole creation groans and labors with birth pangs together until now.

Jesus is chief among those earnestly expecting the revealing of the sons of God. He is very engaged in His own return and literally died for us to have the privilege of contending with Him. Jesus isn't just on an extended sabbatical till His alarm clock goes off! Rather, He is "all-in" interceding for us to wake up and get it together.

Jesus is so serious about contending for us that He is actually fasting in heaven right now. His first miracle was to turn water into wine at a celebration of the wedding. The beginning of His public ministry didn't happen at a wedding by accident, this was a picture of why He came! But the wedding at Cana wasn't the only jaw-dropping story involving Jesus, His beloved friends, and some wine. His last night with His disciples they shared a meal and he poured His last glass of wine:

Matthew 26:29 But I say to you, I will not drink of this fruit of the vine

from now on until that day when I drink it new with you in My Father's kingdom."

This is the heart of a groom. But, it is also supposed to be the heart of a TRUE bride. If my bride, Samantha, was missing from home, there is nothing that would deter me from wanting her back. My life would be on hold until she was back with me, and she would feel the same way about me. This is how Jesus feels about His Bride, and this is how His Bride MUST feel about Him, too. In fact, as Jesus told Ephesus, nothing less than this wholehearted desire will endure.

Jesus is fasting wine until He can drink it with His whole family again on earth. He is contending for us all to be together with Him on earth. This is what God has always wanted: man with God face to face on earth. Until then, earth is broken. In the final years leading up to Jesus' return, the Bride will wake up to this reality and love her groom enough to make this what her life is all about.

But, that waking up...that coming into love...it isn't an emotion, it is a choice. This isn't about evaluating the strength of your love. No one is "there" yet. We all have to wrestle out what this looks like as His appearance unfolds. Jesus' return is a process, on purpose. It is perfectly designed to give the right context for the people of the earth to decide if they are about this wedding, or if they are about what the rest of the world is clamoring for. If you hang onto the world, you will share in the tragic events the world must face. If you hang onto the Groom, you will share in the Groom's life more and more and His return proceeds and the process unfolds.

The length of time for the process if 2,520 days, or 7 prophetic years called the Tribulation. Like any other wedding, the days leading up to the big event are pretty intense. Two families are coming together, and the Bride's side...well, let's just say they need to adjust to the Grooms view of life. The Bible uses hundreds of chapters to describe this process, and, if you study those chapters, you will see it is happening right before our eyes.

The trouble is supposed to make us long for Jesus to return. When we see our brothers and sisters martyred in Smyrna, it is supposed to wake us up to cry out "how long??!!"

Luke 18:7-8 And shall God not avenge His own elect who cry out day and night to Him, though He bears long with them? I tell you that He will avenge them speedily. Nevertheless, when the Son of Man comes, will He really find faith on the earth?"

The process unfolding is also supposed to cause us to begin evaluating our mode of living. It is supposed to cause us to respond in our day to day choices, to grow in love and anticipation.

It takes time to grow in love to the point where you put life on hold until Jesus returns. We must know the Word, as Jesus instructed Pergamos. It must begin by recognizing and then believing that you are actually in THAT day. This is what all of the first disciples did:

1 John 2:18 Little children, it is the last hour; and as you have heard that the Antichrist is coming, even now many antichrists have come, by which we know that it is the last hour.

It is a judgment on this generation that we are actually in the last hour and few will even enter in to what that really means. The corruption of Thyatira must be cast out. Sanctification is what will produce a spotless and pure Bride. She makes herself ready.

You must get ready like you would for any other wedding. Everything else needs to be put on hold until the wedding happens. Sifting your beliefs and your choices is what makes you ready to endure. This wedding is going to have some trouble, and, if you are a believer pretty much anywhere but North America, you are already feeling it. The sifting of the Bride IS coming here, friends:

Matthew 24:9-13 "Then they will deliver you up to tribulation and kill you, and you will be hated by all nations for My name's sake. 10 And then many will be offended, will betray one another, and will hate one another. 11 Then many false prophets will rise up and deceive many. 12 And because lawlessness will abound, the love of many will grow cold. 13 But he who endures to the end shall be saved.

You get ready over time. You wouldn't try to do all your wedding prep on the day of your natural wedding, because it would be more important to you than that. Why would you take a wait and see approach to a much more important wedding than the earthly one you put everything into?

Day by day, it is the choice to wrestle with what you see and what you pick to invest yourself in next. As we grow intentionally grow into the reality of the hour, it makes us ready as we choose to forgo life now for a life that lives longing for Him to return. This requires the Spirit of life to breath real life into us, like Sardis so desperately needs. We want lives filled with the fascination of studying the events of Jesus' return so we can do anything possible to hasten the day.

If my wife disappeared, nothing would deter me from doing whatever it takes to get her back. Night and day I would search for her with all my strength. Jesus feels this way about His Bride. His Bride must feel this way about Him, and will before He returns. That is the Philadelphian promise for not only protection, but to be called faithful! The lovesick Bride will cry "come" as a main occupation, while still living life.

It is actually the "normal" dynamic of the return of Jesus that makes coming out of the world and into that "end time reality" SO hard, but that is the point. You actually have to choose which life you want.

Which life do YOU want?

Matthew 24:37-39 But as the days of Noah were, so also will the coming of the Son of Man be. 38 For as in the days before the flood, they were eating and drinking, marrying and giving in marriage, until the day that Noah entered the ark, 39 and did not know until the flood came and took them all away, so also will the coming of the Son of Man be.

Many, especially in the present-day Church, are sickeningly lukewarm like Laodicea. Jesus would actually prefer cold to lukewarm, because Jesus would prefer you spend yourself on what you REALLY want! It is hard to believe something no one around you seems to believe and then begin making PRACTICAL choices about what you do and say that reflect your unpopular belief. The practical working out of this reality is called "buying oil." Every desire that might distract me that I forgo, every plan I alter, every person I contend for by telling them the truth and not just saying I'll pray for them, but actually taking the time to pray for them, every word I speak in truth no matter the consequence -- it not only hastens the day, it makes me ready FOR that day.

Matthew 25:1-13 "Then the kingdom of heaven shall be likened to ten virgins who took their lamps and went out to meet the bridegroom. Now five of them were wise, and five were foolish. Those who were foolish took their lamps and took no oil with them, but the wise took oil in their vessels with their lamps. But while the bridegroom was delayed, they all slumbered and slept. "And at midnight a cry was heard: 'Behold, the bridegroom is coming; go out to meet him!' Then all those virgins arose and trimmed their lamps. And the foolish said to the wise, 'Give us some of your oil, for our lamps are going out.' But the wise answered, saying, ' No, lest there should not be enough for us and you; but go rather to those who sell, and buy for yourselves.' And while they went to buy, the bridegroom came, and those who were ready went in with him to the wedding; and the door was shut.

"Afterward the other virgins came also, saying, 'Lord, Lord, open to us!' But he answered and said, 'Assuredly, I say to you, I do not know you.' "Watch therefore, for you know neither the day nor the hour in which the Son of Man is coming.

Watch. Pray. Be Ready.

...He is coming...

Made in the USA
Lexington, KY
16 January 2015